Food and Festivals of China

Yan Liao

Mason Crest
Philadelphia

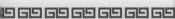

CHINA
THE EMERGING SUPERPOWER

The Ancient History of China

Art and Architecture of China

China Under Reform

The Economy of China

Famous People of China

Food and Festivals of China

The Geography of China

The Government of China

The History of Modern China

The People of China

Food and Festivals of China

Yan Liao

Mason Crest
Philadelphia

Mason Crest
370 Reed Road
Broomall, PA 19008
www.masoncrest.com

CPSIA Compliance Information: Batch #CH2013-6.
For further information, contact Mason Crest at 1-866-MCP-Book.

First printing

1 3 5 7 9 8 6 4 2

Library of Congress Cataloging-in-Publication Data

Liao, Yan.
  Food and festivals of China / Yan Liao.
      p. cm. — (China: the emerging superpower)
  Includes bibliographical references and index.
  ISBN 978-1-4222-2159-4 (hardcover : alk. paper)
  ISBN 978-1-4222-2170-9 (pbk. : alk. paper)
  ISBN 978-1-4222-9448-2 (ebook : alk. paper)
  I. Title.
  GT4883.A2L562 2006
  394.260951—dc22
                                    2010047753

Table of Contents

Introduction

Dr. Jianwei Wang
University of Wisconsin-Stevens Point

Before his first official visit to the United States in December 2003, Chinese premier Wen Jiabao granted a lengthy interview to the *Washington Post*. In that interview, he observed: "If I can speak very honestly and in a straightforward manner, I would say the understanding of China by some Americans is not as good as the Chinese people's understanding of the United States." Needless to say, Mr. Wen was making a sweeping generalization. From my personal experience and observation, some Americans understand China at least as well as some Chinese understand the United States. But overall there remains some truth in Mr. Wen's remarks. For example, if you visited a typical high school in China, you would probably find that students there know more about the United States than their American counterparts know about China. For one thing, most Chinese teenagers start learning English in high school, while only a very small fraction of American high school students will learn Chinese.

In a sense, the knowledge gap between Americans and Chinese about each other is understandable. For the Chinese, the United States is the most important foreign country, representing not just the most developed economy, unrivaled military might, and the most advanced science and technology, but also a very attractive political and value system, which many Chinese admire. But for Americans, China is merely one of many foreign countries. As citizens of the world's sole superpower, Americans naturally feel less compelled to learn from others. The Communist nature of the Chinese polity also gives many Americans pause. This gap of interest in and motivation to learn about the other side could be easily detected by the mere fact that every year tens of thousands of Chinese young men and women apply for a visa to study in the United States. Many of them decide to stay in this country. In comparison, many fewer Americans want to study in China, let alone live in that remote land.

Nevertheless, for better or worse, China is becoming more and more important to the United States, not just politically and economically, but also culturally. Most notably, the size of the Chinese population in the United States has increased steadily. China-made goods as well as Chinese food have become a part of most Americans' daily life. China is now the second-largest trade partner of the United States and will be a huge market for American goods and services. China is also one of the largest creditors, with about $1 trillion in U.S. government securities. Internationally China could either help or hinder American foreign policy in the United Nations, on issues ranging from North Korea to non-proliferation of weapons of mass destruction. In the last century, misperception of this vast country cost the United States dearly in the Korean War and the Vietnam War. On the issue of Taiwan, China and the United States may once again embark on a collision course if both sides are not careful in handling the dispute. Simply put, the state of U.S.-China relations may well shape the future not just for Americans and Chinese, but for the world at large as well.

The purpose of this series, therefore, is to help high school students form an accurate, comprehensive, and balanced understanding of China, past and present, good and bad, success and failure, potential and limit, and culture and state. At least three major images will emerge from various volumes in this series.

First is the image of traditional China. China has the longest continuous civilization in the world. Thousands of years of history produced a rich and sophisticated cultural heritage that still influences today's China. While this ancient civilization is admired and appreciated by many Chinese as well as foreigners, it can also be heavy baggage that makes progress in China difficult and often very costly. This could partially explain why China, once the most advanced country in the world, fell behind during modern times. Foreign encroachment and domestic trouble often plunged this ancient nation into turmoil and war. National rejuvenation and restoration of the historical greatness is still considered the most important mission for the Chinese people today.

Second is the image of Mao's China. The establishment of the People's Republic of China in 1949 marked a new era in this war-torn land. Initially the Communist regime was quite popular and achieved significant accomplishments by bringing order and stability back to Chinese society. When Mao declared that the "Chinese people stood up" at Tiananmen Square, "the sick man of East Asia" indeed reemerged on the world stage as a united and independent power. Unfortunately, Mao soon plunged the country into endless political campaigns that climaxed in the disastrous Cultural Revolution. China slipped further into political suppression, diplomatic isolation, economic backwardness, and cultural stagnation.

Third is the image of China under reform. Mao's era came to an abrupt end after his death in 1976. Guided by Deng Xiaoping's farsighted and courageous policy of reform and openness, China has experienced earth-shaking changes in the last quarter century. With the adoption of a market economy, in just two decades China transformed itself into a global economic powerhouse. China has also become a full-fledged member of the international community, as exemplified by its return to the United Nations and its accession to the World Trade Organization. Although China is far from being democratic as measured by Western standards, overall it is now a more humane place to live, and the Chinese people have begun to enjoy unprecedented freedom in a wide range of social domains.

These three images of China, strikingly different, are closely related with one another. A more sophisticated and balanced perception of China needs to take into consideration all three images and the process of their evolution from one to another, thus acknowledging the great progress China has made while being fully aware that it still has a long way to go. In my daily contact with Americans, I quite often find that their views of China are based on the image of traditional China and of China under Mao—they either discount or are unaware of the dramatic changes that have taken place. Hopefully this series will allow its readers to observe the following realities about China.

First, China is not black and white, but rather—like the United States—complex and full of contradictions. For such a vast country, one or two negative stories in the media often do not represent the whole picture. Surely the economic reforms have reduced many old problems, but they have also created many new problems. Not all of these problems, however, necessarily prove the guilt of the Communist system. Rather, they may be the result of the very reforms the government has been implementing and of the painful transition from one system to another. Those who would view China through a single lens will never fully grasp the complexity of that country.

Second, China is not static. Changes are taking place in China every day. Anyone who lived through Mao's period can attest to how big the changes have been. Every time I return to China, I discover something new. Some things have changed for the better, others for the worse. The point I want to make is that today's China is a very dynamic society. But the development in China has its own pace and logic. The momentum of changes comes largely from within rather than from without. Americans can facilitate but not dictate such changes.

Third, China is neither a paradise nor a hell. Economically China is still a developing country with a very low per capita GDP because of its huge population. As the Chinese premier put it, China may take another 100 years to catch up with the United States. China's political system remains authoritarian and can be repressive and arbitrary. Chinese people still do not have as much freedom as American people enjoy, particularly when it comes to expressing opposition to the government. So China is certainly not an ideal society, as its leaders used to believe (or at least declare). Yet the Chinese people as a whole are much better off today than they were 25 years ago, both economically and politically. Chinese authorities were fond of telling the Chinese people that Americans lived in an abyss of misery. Now every Chinese knows that this is nonsense. It is equally ridiculous to think of the Chinese in a similar way.

Finally, China is both different from and similar to the United States. It is true that the two countries differ greatly in terms of political and social systems and cultural tradition. But it is also true that China's program of reform and openness has made these two societies much more similar. China is largely imitating the United States in many aspects. One can easily detect the convergence of the two societies in terms of popular culture, values, and lifestyle by walking on the streets of Chinese cities like Shanghai. With ever-growing economic and other functional interactions, the two countries have also become increasingly interdependent. That said, it is naïve to expect that China will become another United States. Even if China becomes a democracy one day, these two great nations may still not see eye to eye on many issues.

Understanding an ancient civilization and a gigantic country such as China is always a challenge. If this series kindles readers' interest in China and provides them with systematic information and thoughtful perspectives, thus assisting their formation of an informed and realistic image of this fascinating country, I am sure the authors of this series will feel much rewarded.

Lions, dragons, and other colorful creatures populate parades held to celebrate Chinese holidays. Learning about China's traditional festivals and holidays can help further a better understanding of Chinese culture.

Overview: Windows to Culture

"When entering a country, ask what the customs are." This old Chinese saying can certainly be seen as sensible, practical advice for getting along in an unfamiliar land. But it represents more than that, for customs can reveal much about the essence of a people and their culture.

One custom that is common across cultures is the holding of festivals, holidays, and other celebrations at regular times during the year. On the most basic level, these observances serve as welcome breaks from the routines of daily life. On another level, though, they often carry deeper meanings, incorporating and reflecting aspects of a society's unique history, social conventions, and beliefs. For the careful observer, the traditional festival in particular can serve as a window to a better understanding of another culture.

An Ancient Civilization

China boasts one of the world's longest continuous civilizations, and many of its traditional festivals can be traced back 3,000 or even 4,000 years. Most have origins in one or more legendary stories.

In the Chinese creation myth, the universe begins with a powerful being named Pangu (spelled "P'an-ku" in the old system for transliterating Chinese characters). With his mighty ax, Pangu separates the chaos at the beginning of time into sky and earth, and thus creates life. Pangu is followed by a series of legendary heroes and kings, who, through their various deeds, form the nation that will eventually become known as China.

The archaeological record of Chinese civilization begins with the Xia (Hsia) dynasty, which existed more than 2,000 years before the birth of Christ and which, until the latter half of the 20th century, was thought to be entirely mythical. When the Chinese consider the four millennia of their civilization's history, dynasties frequently provide the frame of reference. From the Xia to the present, China counts a dozen major dynasties (and many more minor ones), along with four important periods. The last Chinese dynasty, the Qing (Ch'ing), was overthrown in 1911. It was followed by the Republic of China, which was in turn replaced in 1949 by the People's Republic of China.

Traditional Chinese Festivals

Traditional Chinese festivals are observed according to the lunar calendar, which is based on the cycles of the moon. Each month begins on a new moon and consists of 29 or 30 days. One lunar year is made up of 12 months (or 13 in the case of a leap year, which occurs about once every three years). Chinese people commonly refer to their lunar calendar as the agricultural calendar, because farmers have used it to determine the right time for planting, harvesting, and other agricultural activities since the reign of the Xia dynasty, some 4,000 years ago. The Western, or Gregorian, calendar was not adopted in China until after the fall of the Qing dynasty in 1911.

Because of the length of China's history and the vastness of its territory (in total area China and the United States are approximately the same size), numerous festivals and celebrations fill the Chinese calendar. Some are observed by the whole nation, while others are particular to one province or even one village. Of those that are celebrated by all Chinese, the most important are three "festivals of the living." There are also three "festivals of the dead," a festival of romance, and a festival of family survival. Certain details of these festivals—for example, the foods that are eaten—vary somewhat by region. But the major elements, such as an emphasis on family and respect for ancestors, are the same for Chinese everywhere. This includes many of the millions of overseas Chinese—even those whose families left China generations ago. Whether they now live in Southeast Asia or South America, in Europe, North America, or Australia, most ethnic Chinese maintain connections to their cultural heritage. And this means celebrating the traditional festivals.

Because China has historically been an agricultural nation, the dates of most traditional festivals and ceremonies are established by the lunar calendar, which originally helped farmers determine the best time to plant and harvest.

A poster of Mao Zedong (1893–1976) overlooks Tiananmen Square, Beijing. The Chinese observe National Day on October 1, to commemorate the day in 1949 when Mao proclaimed the establishment of the People's Republic of China.

Official Holidays

The traditional festivals discussed in this book have all been observed for hundreds, if not thousands, of years. Some of them, such as the Ghost Festival, started as religious celebrations, but the religious aspect is long lost. While Buddhism and Taoism deeply influenced Chinese culture, they never dominated the everyday life of the Chinese, as Christianity did in Western culture. Chinese festivals are essentially family festivals rather than church or state festivals.

Of course, China has always had state holidays. In the past, an emperor would designate his birthday as the official holiday for the country. However, when a new emperor took over, that holiday would invariably be replaced with the new emperor's birthday. Today, major official holidays in China include National Day, observed on October 1 to celebrate the 1949 establishment of the People's Republic of China. The first of May is International Labor Day (not to be confused with Labor Day in the United States). New Year's Day on the Western calendar (January 1) is also an official holiday in China. Most of these state holidays, however, are not real festivals to the Chinese, who regard them more as days off work than occasions for celebration. In recent years, Western festivals such as Christmas and Halloween, along with certain holidays such as Mother's Day, have also entered Chinese life and are becoming popular in big cities, which is but another manifestation of today's global village.

Ethnic Festivals

The term *Chinese*, when used in a cultural or ethnic context, commonly refers to the Han people, who make up more than 90 percent of China's population. Thus, Chinese traditional festivals come from the traditions and culture of the Han, who take their

Major Dynasties and Periods in Chinese History

Ca. 2100–ca. 1600 B.C.	Xia (Hsia)
Ca. 1600–ca. 1028 B.C.	Shang
Ca. 1027–771 B.C.	Western Zhou (Chou)
771–221 B.C.	Eastern Zhou
	Spring and Autumn Period
	Warring States Period
221–206 B.C.	Qin (Ch'in)
206 B.C.–A.D. 220	Eastern and Western Han
581–618	Sui
618–907	Tang (T'ang)
960–1279	Northern and Southern Song (Sung)
1260–1368	Yuan (Yüan)
1368–1644	Ming
1644–1911	Qing (Ch'ing)
1911–1949	Republic of China
1949–present	People's Republic of China

name from the famous Han dynasty (206 B.C.–A.D. 220). In the political sense, however, the word *Chinese* embraces 55 ethnic groups, in addition to the Han, who live within the People's Republic of China. These 55 groups, officially referred to as "national minorities," occupy 50 to 60 percent of the country's total land area, but account for less than 10 percent of the population. They live in the grasslands of the north (the Mongolians), in the desert areas of the northwest (the Uighurs), on the great plateau of the west (the Tibetans), and in the mountainous regions of the southwest (Yi, Dai, and many others). Each of these 55 ethnic minorities has its own distinct culture and traditions, and their festivals are as colorful and interesting as those of the Han. Some are very similar to what the Han celebrate (for example, the Tibetan New Year), and others are quite different (the Mongolian Nadam Fair, the Yi people's Torch Festival, and the Dai people's Water Splashing Festival). This book devotes its last chapter to these four ethnic festivals, with the hope of offering a glimpse of the fascinating ethnic cultures in China.

A youth eats a bowl of noodles at an outdoor food stall in Shanghai. Food plays a prominent role in Chinese culture.

Chinese Food

Today very few people are complete strangers to Chinese food, owing to the large number of Chinese restaurants all over the world. Pleasure in food has always been a very important part of the Chinese culture, as reflected in a famous Chinese saying dating to around 200 B.C.: "To ordinary people, food is tantamount to heaven."

Throughout the long history of China, food has gone beyond the means of sustenance and has assumed great importance in tradition, folklore, mythology, ritual, and religious observance. Food helps bind families and friends together. For the Chinese, no social gathering is complete without a good meal, and family reunions are always celebrated with good food. The great philosopher Confucius observed that the enjoyment of food is one of the ways to bring about peace and harmony in society. In his view, the cultivated man should be as concerned with the order, beauty, and harmony of the food on his table as with the affairs of state. Practicing what he preached, Confucius was said to have divorced his wife for her failure in good cooking, and he refused to eat meat that was not properly cut.

The importance of food in the Chinese culture is registered in everyday language. A person who bumps into a friend on the street is very likely to be greeted with "Have you eaten?" rather than "How are you?"—the logic being that having just eaten means a person should be feeling fine and happy. (The conventional response to the greeting is yes, whether or not the person has actually eaten recently.) Rice, the staple food for most Chinese, is also an expression of financial security in the language. "Having grains to chew" means having a job. A person who has "found a rice bowl" has found a job; a person who "broke his rice bowl" has just lost his job. An "iron rice bowl" refers to secure employment.

Ingredients of Chinese Food

When it comes to what constitutes the Chinese diet, there is a popular saying: "Chinese people eat everything flying in the sky except airplanes, everything running on the ground except cars, and everything swimming in the ocean except submarines." This is of course an exaggeration. Nonetheless, it reflects the wide range of ingredients used in Chinese cooking. Sea cucumbers, shark fins, and snakes are among the dishes Western people find most exotic. However, it is a common misunderstanding that Chinese food centers on unusual fare. The truth is that Chinese cuisine shares most basic ingredients found in Western cuisine, such as pork, fish, and various vegetables. The differences between the two reside not so much in the ingredients as in the way the ingredients are prepared.

In southern China, the staple food is rice; in the north, it is wheat.

The most popular meat in Chinese cuisine is pork. Chicken and duck are also among the favorites. Beef is less readily available, largely because oxen still have significant value to farmers and peasants as draft animals. Except for a few minority groups such as the Mongolians and Tibetans, dairy products like cheese and butter are almost nonexistent in the Chinese diet.

Overall, meat is used sparingly in traditional Chinese cooking. It is often cut into small pieces and cooked with other ingredients as a flavoring rather than a main ingredient. In their daily diet the Chinese are accustomed to eating small amounts of meat with lots of vegetables, and most would find it difficult to consume the 12-ounce steaks common on Western dinner plates. In recent years, many people have come to recognize the healthful balance of the Chinese diet, partly because of its use of large quantities and varieties of vegetables with small quantities of meat.

Most Chinese would feel uncomfortable with meals that include few or no vegetables. And centuries of Buddhist influence led the Chinese to develop highly nutritious vegetarian dishes that resemble meat dishes in both taste and texture. At many Buddhist temples, such vegetarian meals are served to the delight of pious believers and casual tourists alike. It is truly a marvel how the vegetables and tofu products are made to look and taste just like meat.

To the Chinese, one of the most important criteria in selecting ingredients is freshness. Every city in China has open markets where fresh produce and meat are sold unpackaged and unprocessed. People buy their food from these markets daily. When it comes to meat, the Chinese idea of freshness is rather different from that of Westerners. To the Chinese, getting truly fresh meat frequently entails buying a live animal. While it is difficult to keep a live pig in the kitchen, chicken and fish are often sold alive

Fresh ingredients are an important element of Chinese cooking. In cities shoppers can purchase fresh fruits and vegetables, as well as live chickens or fish, at open-air markets.

and butchered right before cooking to ensure freshness. Huge fish tanks with live fish, shrimp, and lobsters are a common sight in Chinese restaurants—and patrons shouldn't mistake them for the restaurant décor.

Traditional Chinese cooking depends heavily on lard (fat from pork) for its rich flavor and clear color. Today the more health conscious are likely to use vegetable oil instead. Popular vegetable oils include canola, peanut, and corn; olive oil is only a recent import from Western countries.

Cooking the Food

In China, cooking—even for the most accomplished chefs— involves improvising with the ingredients on hand; and feel and taste, rather than recipes, dictate the approach to preparing food. For the Chinese, the idea of exact time (seconds, minutes, or hours) and quantities (spoons, cups, or pounds) in cooking is a rather alien concept. In fact, timers, measuring cups, and measuring spoons won't be found in a traditional Chinese kitchen. Nor will a Chinese cook asked how he or she makes a particular dish respond with clear, written amounts of ingredients and an exact cooking time, for such concrete instructions are almost nonexistent in the world of Chinese cuisine.

Making Chinese food can be very time-consuming. One reason is that the preparation before the actual cooking takes a lot of time, as ingredients for the same dish are typically cut into uniform shapes, and preferably into bite-sized pieces. For example, diced

FAST FACTS

About Chinese Cuisine

- The staple food is rice in the South and wheat in the North.
- Banquet dinners typically run more than a dozen courses.
- Soup comes last in a meal.
- Chinese people believe that some foods can heat the body and others can cool it.
- Most Chinese restaurants overseas represent the cooking style from only one Chinese province.

meat requires that the accompanying vegetables also be diced; likewise, if the meat is sliced, the vegetables should be sliced.

Chinese cooking employs different methods according to the nature of the ingredients, the degree of heat, and the length of cooking time. The major emphasis, though, is on enhancing the natural flavor of ingredients, as well as retaining nutrients.

Stir-frying is one of the most popular cooking methods. It is similar to sautéing: ingredients are fried in a small amount of oil, over high heat and with constant stirring. The bite-sized ingredients allow for quick cooking (usually only a few minutes), and more important, the meat and vegetables retain their juices, tenderness, and nutrients.

Almost every Chinese kitchen has a bamboo steamer, as steaming is another popular method in Chinese cooking. In this method, foods are put in the steamer above boiling water and are cooked by the heat of the water vapor. This technique preserves the colors, flavors, and nutrients of the ingredients.

Hongshao (hung shao), or red stewing, is a unique Chinese method achieved by stewing food in large quantities of soy sauce and water. The soy sauce gives the food an appetizing reddish brown color and a rich taste. Red stewing is usually used for meat dishes such as pork, beef, chicken, and duck.

Among the many other cooking methods used are boiling, shallow frying, and deep frying. It is common to use more than one technique in preparing a single dish. For example, pork may be deep-fried first and then red-stewed or steamed. A good cook knows which techniques to use to combine the natural flavors of the ingredients for the best taste and nutrition.

Dining

Westerners are often surprised at the number of courses at a Chinese banquet—typically more than a dozen. Such party dishes are served at an interval of a few minutes. Chinese people don't

Steaming food—such as this fresh corn on the cob—is a popular method of cooking in China, and most kitchens have a bamboo steamer.

usually entertain guests at home for such party meals—they take them to restaurants—but if they do, they prepare the same kind of banquet. It is customary for the hosts to provide much more than can be eaten, as a way of showing their hospitality. In fact, if everything were finished on the dinner table, the hosts would feel embarrassed and would apologize for the "meager" food.

Family meals, on the other hand, are smaller in scale. They might consist of four dishes and a soup. And unlike at a banquet, at a family meal all dishes are served at the same time for everybody to enjoy.

At the Chinese dinner table, each person has his or her own bowl of the staple food (rice or, in northern China, wheat). Unlike many Americans, the Chinese would never pour soy sauce on their rice to flavor it. Rice should be enjoyed in its own right, and the meat

A farming family, seated around the dinner table, eats a meal at their home.

and vegetable dishes serve as its flavoring. On the Chinese dinner table, one will not find shakers for salt and pepper—or any other spices or sauces, for that matter—because every dish is supposed to come well seasoned. Because meat and vegetables are already cut into bite-sized pieces, chopsticks suffice in transporting the food from the plate into the mouth. In fact, the Chinese would find knives on the dinner table unacceptable and even "barbarous."

Chinese dinner tables are usually round. This serves two functions: it puts each diner at the same distance from the meat and vegetable dishes placed in the center of the table, and it allows for general conversation among all diners. Plates and bowls are typically round also, as roundness is a symbol of harmony and family togetherness in the Chinese culture. (By contrast, in Japan and some other Asian countries, containers of different shapes are used to accommodate different food for an aesthetic appeal.) On the Chinese table, a dish is never passed. People use chopsticks to take what they want from the dishes at the center of the table.

Soup is usually the concluding dish in a Chinese meal, and traditionally there is no dessert other than fresh fruit. One is supposed to finish the staple food in his or her own bowl, as a way of honoring rice and wheat as the staff of life, but it is all right to leave the meat and vegetable dishes unfinished.

Regional Food

Dining out at a Chinese restaurant in the United States differs somewhat from eating a typical meal in China. At the Chinese restaurant, for example, soup is served first rather than last, and at the end of the meal fortune cookies are distributed. Beyond that, though, most Americans are not aware that the overwhelming majority of Chinese restaurants in the United States represent only one of the many distinct regional styles of cooking in China: the Cantonese style. (In the Chinatowns of major U.S. cities, however, diners can find increasingly diversified forms of Chinese cuisine.) The dominance of Cantonese food stems from the fact that almost all early Chinese immigrants were from the province of Canton (now called Guangdong), in southern China.

At the broadest level, Chinese cuisine can be divided into four major schools—Northeast, East, Southeast, and Southwest—based primarily on climate, temperament of the people, and foods generally available in quantity. The brief descriptions that follow don't do justice to the incredible variety of regional cooking in China. But, it is hoped, the reader will get a sense of the richness of Chinese cuisine.

The Northeast school of Chinese cuisine (often also referred to as classic or mandarin cuisine) covers the northeastern area of China, including Beijing, Tianjin, Hebei, Henan, and Shandong. Wheat noodles and steamed bread and buns are the staple food in this area. Meat such as lamb, mutton, and beef also constitutes a big part of the diet—a fact attributable largely to the proximity with Inner Mongolia, which has vast expanses of grassland for grazing

A chef prepares food in the kitchen of a restaurant in Guangzhou. The Cantonese style of Chinese cooking is just one of several regional styles, but it is the one most familiar to Americans.

animals. Seasoning in the Northeast school of cuisine is generally mild, but sauces tend to be rich. The most famous dishes in this school are Peking roast duck and *jiaozi (chiao tzu)*, boiled or steamed dumplings with meat and vegetable fillings.

The East style is the major school of cuisine in China's eastern coastal area. The area, which includes Shanghai, Zhejiang, and Jiangsu, is blessed with rich soil and good irrigation systems from the Yangtze River. Rice is the staple food here, and the vegetarian dishes are famous. The diet also incorporates a variety of freshwater fish and seafood. Eastern China's cuisine is probably most famous for its dainty snacks and pastries such as crabmeat buns. People in this area like to add sugar to every dish they cook.

Southeast cuisine is represented by Canton, which, as mentioned earlier, is the best-known style of Chinese cooking outside China.

A climate of mild winters and plentiful rainfall, combined with fertile land, gives this region a huge variety of vegetables and fruits. Seafood here is also excellent. Southeast Chinese cuisine uses the widest range of ingredients, including two of the most famous, shark fin and bird's nest. Dim sum—delightful dumplings and buns filled with meat, seafood, sweetened bean mixtures, bamboo shoots, and mushrooms—is one of the best-liked foods from this regional cooking.

Southwestern China is a subtropical area that includes Sichuan, Guizhou, Yunnan, and Hunan. For most outsiders, the outstanding—or perhaps overwhelming—feature of Southwest Chinese cuisine is its spicy hotness. Hot chili pepper is used very liberally in the cooking, and so is the Sichuan peppercorn, which can numb the mouth and tongue. People from outside this region often find the very spicy dishes intimidating at first. Given time, however, many come to love Southwest cuisine. Famous dishes from this style include Ma-p'o tofu and twice-cooked pork.

Food as Medicine

For centuries, the Chinese have recognized a close link between food and health. They believe that everything a person eats and drinks has an effect on his or her *qi (ch'i)*, the "vital energy" in the body. Certain foods can heat the body's *qi*, while other foods can cool it. Rich and oily food, fatty meat, heavily spiced food, and strong alcohol are among the former group, and bland or bitter-tasting food such as most vegetables and watery fruits are among the latter. When the body's *qi* is in balance, a person is healthy and energetic. Consuming too much "heating" food can cause the body's *qi* to become too "hot" (a hangover is a good example). When that happens, a person should eat "cooling" foods and avoid "heating" foods so as to restore the balance of *qi* and return to health. On the other hand, when the *qi* in the body is too "cold," a person typically feels a lack of energy. In that case the right thing to do is eat more "heating" foods to restore the balance of *qi*. Because of the belief in *qi*, when Chinese people become sick their first remedy is typically an examination of their diet and an adjustment of what they eat.

Many of the plants commonly used in Chinese cooking have known value in preventing and alleviating illnesses. These include spring onion (scallions), gingerroot, garlic, lotus seeds, and tree fungus (wood ears). The Chinese make good use of these medicinal plants, as shown in a home remedy for the common cold: ginger soup (gingerroot boiled with brown sugar). Cantonese cuisine is especially famous for its use of medicinal plants and herbs in everyday cooking. Belief in the remedial and preventive value of medicinal food is still prevalent—the Chinese have always insisted that "remedy from medicine is never as good as remedy from food"—and one can find restaurants specializing in medicinal food in major Chinese cities.

Food for Celebrations

Food is an essential part of traditional Chinese festivals honoring ancestors and gods, celebrating family togetherness, and commemorating historical figures or events. As will be discussed in the following chapters, many Chinese festivals are associated with special types of food and treats. For the Spring Festival, or the Chinese New Year, people eat all kinds of foods with auspicious names or meanings, such as tangerines (which sound the same as the word for "good luck" in Chinese) and fish (which connotes overflowing happiness and fortune). At the Dragon Boat Festival, people make *zongzi*, a rice dumpling with sweet or savory fillings, to commemorate a patriotic poet from more than 2,000 years ago. And moon cakes are a special treat at the Mid-Autumn Festival, which celebrates the beautiful full moon.

Many foods have acquired special cultural meanings over the course of China's long history. Peaches stand for immortality or long life, for example, and are always dedicated to the elders. Pomegranates, with their numerous seeds, represent the blessings of many sons, which is much valued in the Chinese culture. Noodles are associated with birthdays, as their length symbolizes longevity.

Chinese office workers rehearse a dragon dance routine outside their building, in preparation for the Chinese New Year celebrations. The Spring Festival is the most significant of all Chinese festivals.

3

The Spring Festival

The Spring Festival, or *Chun Jie (Ch'un Chieh)*, is the Chinese New Year. Celebrated on the first day of the first lunar month, it is not only the first of the three "festivals of the living" but also the most significant of all Chinese festivals. Today, the Chinese actually celebrate two New Years: the Chinese New Year and the New Year on the Western calendar. "Spring Festival" is a modern term that distinguishes the former from the latter, which is called *Yuandan (Yüan Tan)*. For thousands of years, the lunar calendar was the only one in use in China, and when people spoke of Yuandan, they meant the lunar New Year. After China's last dynasty was swept from power in 1911, the Republic of China government officially adopted the Gregorian calendar. Since then, the term *Yuandan* has been reserved for the Western New Year, whereas the Chinese New Year has become the Spring

Festival, as it always falls right before or after the Chinese solar term designated *Lichun (Li Ch'un)*, or "the Beginning of Spring." (In traditional China, a solar term is a period of time equivalent to 1/24th of a year.)

The Chinese New Year starts on the second new moon after the winter solstice (December 21 or 22); on the Western calendar, it usually falls between late January and early February. This is the coldest time of the year, and in many areas the conditions are anything but springlike. Nonetheless, nature is waking up amidst the snow, and growth is in the air. Chinese people celebrate this time with the most colorful, sensational, and joyous festival of the year.

In one way, the Spring Festival is to the Chinese as Thanksgiving is to Americans: it centers on family. People journey home and gather with their families to eat, drink, rejoice in one another's company, and honor their ancestors. However, the Spring Festival lasts much longer than Thanksgiving. Traditionally, people start the preparations one month before the festival, and the celebrations do not officially end until *Yuanxiao Jie (Yüan Hsiao Chieh)*, the Lantern Festival, which comes on the 15th day of the lunar New Year. Today Chinese people enjoy a week off from work during the Spring Festival.

The Month of Preparation

The 12th month of the Chinese year is called *La Yue (La Yüeh)*, the Month of Offerings. This is the month of preparation for the Spring Festival, during which people reflect on the past year, clean the house, offer sacrifices to gods, and drive away evil spirits.

In the Chinese folk culture, there are as many gods as there are humans. Like officials in a government, the Chinese gods each have duties in the human world and oversee different aspects of human behavior. Such a relationship between humans and gods is said to have been the origin of the Spring Festival. One time in the remote past, a household god was offended by the misbehaviors of his earthly subjects. Upon his return to heaven, the angry god suggested to the Jade Emperor, the supreme ruler of all Chinese gods, that the earth be destroyed. However, other gods had enjoyed their dealings with humans and didn't want such a thing to happen. They urged the Jade Emperor to make a personal inspection and decide for himself. These gods also warned people on earth of the inspection beforehand. To please the Jade Emperor and his entourage, people stopped their daily routines, tidied up their everyday affairs, and presented lavish food and drink offerings to the gods. When the Jade Emperor saw a harmonious human world with respect for the gods above, he decided not to destroy the earth. To commemorate this happy outcome, it is said, people started to hold an annual celebration, which gradually became a festival lasting well over a month.

The first important festive activity in the "month of preparation" happens on the eighth day, when most families cook *laba zhou (la pa chou)*, a sweet porridge made of rice or other grains with a mixture of nuts and dried fruits such as walnuts, pine seeds, gingko, peanuts, lotus seeds, persimmons, and dates. The custom of eating *laba zhou* has its origins in a Buddhist tradition: on the eighth day of the 12th month, many Buddhist temples would distribute the porridge, to celebrate the achieving of enlightenment by Sakyamuni, the founder of Buddhism. However, like many other Chinese traditions, it has long lost any religious meaning, and for ordinary families this day is no more than an occasion to enjoy the sweet and nutritious gruel during the cold winter. People present homemade *laba zhou* to friends and relatives to share the festive spirit.

During the month of preparation, all Chinese families busy themselves cleaning house. This housecleaning is much like the spring cleaning in the United States, but it has the special meaning of "sweeping out the old, and welcoming in the new." Every corner of the house is swept, every piece of furniture wiped down, and every article of stored clothing aired. It is believed that all the misfortunes and unhappiness that have accumulated during the past year will disappear with the dust and dirt. Even the boldest demons dare not enter a clean household.

On the 23rd (in some areas the 24th) day of the 12th month, a special ceremony called "sending off the Kitchen God" is performed in the family kitchen. As noted earlier, Chinese gods, like the staff of a government's ministries, are appointed to various posts and duties. In the last month of the year, they all go up to heaven and report to the Jade Emperor on their activities. This, for the most part, does not concern humans.

When it comes to the Kitchen God, however, things are a little different. This household deity, whose presence is represented by a small picture above the kitchen stove, stays with the family year round. Nevertheless, he receives little attention over the course of the year, enjoying no more than the smoke and vapor that come from cooking. But this petty god suddenly becomes an important figure on the 23rd of the 12th month, for when he goes up to heaven the Kitchen God is responsible for reporting the good and bad deeds of the family to the Jade Emperor. Based on this report, the Jade Emperor allocates the family's portion of happiness and fortune, which the Kitchen God then brings back to the household.

The Kitchen God has lived with the family for the whole year and has seen and heard everything. What if he were to present an unfavorable account of the family's deeds? The days of a family member might well be shortened, or the luck and fortune of the entire family taken away. While this seems like an unsettling prospect, the Chinese don't worry too much. As is the case with humans, there are always ways to win the gods' hearts.

When the day comes for the Kitchen God to go up to heaven, the

This painting, on display in a museum in Canada, shows a procession of major Chinese deities. In the center are the Lord of the Southern Dipper, the Jade Emperor, and the Empress of Heaven.

family lays out for him sacrifices in the form of various sweets, such as cakes and candied fruit. The family also smears his mouth with honey. After such a sweet farewell meal, it is believed, only sweet remarks can come from his lips. This is sheer bribery, but neither the people nor the Kitchen God seems to mind. Sometimes sweet sticky rice is even included in the offerings, the aim being to seal the lips of the Kitchen God so he won't be able to talk at all when he goes to see the Jade Emperor.

After the food is offered with words of praise and good wishes, the Kitchen God's picture is taken to the family courtyard, where it is burnt as a way of sending him up to heaven. Paper horses and paper spirit money are also burnt to make his journey pleasant. A few days later, on New Year's Eve, a new picture of the Kitchen God will be posted above the family stove, and this compassionate deity will again oversee the family business in the coming year.

As the New Year approaches, the festive atmosphere grows stronger and stronger. The period of the Spring Festival is rich in sound and color (in particular, the color red). The ear-piercing sound of firecrackers can be heard everywhere, and red is used in various kinds of decorations.

Setting off firecrackers is a tradition handed down from the ancient past, when people burnt bamboo stems. (Bamboo sticks have joints with hollows in between, and when burned, the joints burst open and produce a loud popping sound.) Various legends seek to explain the origins of this tradition. One tells of a monster that hid in the mountains and came out to kill people and their livestock at the end of every year. After many futile attempts to kill it, people found out by chance that this savage creature was afraid of loud noise, light, and the color red. So when the monster appeared again, they painted their doors red and burned some bamboo stems. The color red and the loud noise made by the bamboo stems frightened the monster so much that he ran his head off to escape, never returning to harm the people again. Later, when gunpowder was invented in China, the bamboo stems were replaced with firecrackers, but the term *baozhu (pao chu)*, which means "burning bamboo," remains in use today as a name for firecrackers.

Over the centuries, the tradition of setting off firecrackers has entered the everyday life of the Chinese. It is a popular way to celebrate, not only during the Spring Festival but also during other joyous occasions, such as shop openings and weddings. In recent years, however, the Chinese government has tried to ban firecrackers in cities because they frequently cause fires and injuries, particularly during the Spring Festival.

The color red enjoys a special status in the Chinese culture. It represents happiness and good luck and is used in many celebratory occasions. For example, the traditional Chinese bride wears a red wedding dress, and her wedding chamber is also decorated in red. During the Spring Festival, red can repel evil spirits and bring good luck. Every household posts red pictures of Door Gods; red spring couplets; a red diamond-shaped "fortune" character; and, in northern China, red "papercuts"—pieces of paper artfully cut into intricate patterns. Children receive money in *hongbao (hung pao)*, "the red envelopes," and people wear red clothes.

The Door Gods, which Chinese put on the center panel of the front entrance to their houses, especially in the countryside, are the images of two husky, tough-looking generals from hundreds of years ago. They are Qin Qiong (Ch'in Ch'iung) and Yuchi Gong (Yü-ch'i Kung) from the Tang dynasty (A.D. 618–907). Legend has it that Emperor Taizong (T'ai-tsung), who had fought numerous battles during the course of establishing China's most powerful and prosperous dynasty, once found his dreams haunted by ghosts. For days he was unable to sleep peacefully. When two of his generals, Qin Qiong and Yuchi Gong, learned this, they told the emperor that they would stand guard outside his bedchamber to keep the ghosts away. That night the two generals, carrying weapons and dressed in full armor, kept watch as they had promised. No ghost appeared in the emperor's dreams, and he awoke the next day refreshed and happy. But instead of asking his two favorite generals to stand guard all night again, the emperor had pictures of them painted on red paper and posted these pictures on his bedchamber doors. The ghosts never returned to haunt him. When people heard about the story, they started posting pictures of the two generals on

The Chinese are credited with creating firecrackers thousands of years ago. Then, as now, firecrackers were used to frighten away evil spirits and celebrate holidays.

their own doors, hoping that this would protect their families against evil spirits and ghosts too. And posting Door Gods has since been part of the Spring Festival traditions.

Chun lian (ch'un lien), or the spring couplet, is two lines of verse, written on red paper in black or golden ink and used as a decoration during the Spring Festival. Its theme usually involves people's good wishes for the New Year, and structurally each word and phrase from the first line of the couplet has a corresponding word or phrase in the second. Spring couplets are posted in various places in the house: on the front door beside the Door Gods, in the living room, or by the family altar.

The first spring couplet was created by a king of the Later Shu (A.D. 934–965). As translated in Xing Qi's book *Folk Customs at Traditional Chinese Festivals* (Beijing: Foreign Languages Press, 1988), it reads: "A new year to take in surplus fortune/A fine festival to call in eternal spring."

Spring couplets originated from the so-called peachwood charms used in ancient times. These were rectangular plates, made from the wood of peach trees, that had magic charms written or drawn on them. Peach has long been an auspicious wood in the Chinese culture. Its strong scent is believed to have evil-repelling power. The early Chinese hung peachwood charms on their doors to drive away demons and invite blessings from the gods. After paper was invented, peachwood charms gradually transformed into the spring couplets we know today, and the charms were replaced with verses that express good wishes.

In the past, scholars accomplished in poetry and the art of writing would compose and write spring couplets for friends and family during the Spring Festival. Today, spring couplets are mass-produced and have lost much of the originality, but they remain a favorite in Chinese households during this festive season.

Besides spring couplets, people also post a special Chinese charac-

ter in their homes. This character is *fu* (seen at right), which means "fortune" or "blessings." It is typically written on a piece of red, diamond-shaped paper, and is often purposely posted upside down. This is because the Chinese word for "upside down," *dao (tao)*, sounds the same as the word for "arrive." By posting *fu* upside down, people express the wish that fortune and blessings will soon arrive.

New Year's Eve

For the Chinese, *Chuxi (Ch'u Hsi)*, New Year's Eve, is reserved exclusively for family. In the days leading up to New Year's Eve, China's roads are jammed with travelers journeying home to join their families in the ceremony of sending off the old year and welcoming in the new one.

The highlight of New Year's Eve is *tuannian fan (t'uan nien fan)*, the Happy Family Reunion Dinner. In old times, a pig was usually slaughtered for the Spring Festival—and for many poorer people, this was the only time when meat was available. Today, freshly made bacon and sausage are hung above the kitchen stove, but housewives cook a variety of dishes for this special celebration. Often they begin their preparations for the Happy Family Reunion Dinner days before New Year's Eve, as many dishes are meant for more than one meal. On the 30th day of the 12th lunar month, every member of the family is home for the biggest dinner of the year. (In the past, three or more generations would gather, though that has been changing in recent times.)

The Happy Family Reunion Dinner is for the ancestors to enjoy first. When all the dishes are ready on the table, the whole family gathers in the living room to perform a ceremony in honor of heaven and earth, various household gods (who by now have returned from their mission of reporting to the Jade Emperor), and the family ancestors.

The head of the family, traditionally the eldest of all the men, leads the ceremony of the night. Sacrifices have by now been laid on the family altar below the ancestor tablets (wooden plaques on which are written the names of the family's ancestors within three generations). Common sacrifices include a pig's head, a whole chicken, and a whole fish. Fresh fruits like oranges and tangerines (both of which represent good luck) are also presented. There are also special pastries, such as peach-like buns—peaches having the auspicious meaning of longevity. Incense is burning on both sides of the altar, and red candles are lit. The head of the family bows to heaven and earth first, then to the various gods, and at last to the family ancestors, chanting wishes for wealth, longevity, and fortune. The rest of the family follows suit and kowtows to the ancestors.

After the sacrifice ceremony, the food is considered to have been "eaten" by the ancestors and is removed from the altar so the living members of the family can enjoy it. The Happy Family Reunion Dinner is the most special meal of the year, and almost every dish comes with an auspicious name for good luck. The Chinese language has a relatively small repertoire of sounds, and thus provides nearly unlimited sources for puns. The Spring Festival is a time filled with puns that are meant to bring fortune and luck.

In North China, the main dish of the Happy Family Reunion Dinner is *jiaozi*, dumplings with meat and vegetable fillings. Because of its shape, *jiaozi* is also called *yuanbao (yüan pao)*, or "money ingot," symbolizing fortune. And when the dumplings are prepared, special objects such as coins are placed inside some of them. People who get the *jiaozi* containing these objects at the dinner table are believed to have the best luck.

In South China, people eat various meat and vegetable dishes instead of *jiaozi* at the Happy Family Reunion Dinner. Chicken and fish are two must-have dishes, because the Chinese word for chicken, *ji (chi)*, has the same pronunciation as the word for "good

People burn incense and pray at the Baiyunguan Taoist temple in Beijing on the first day of the lunar New Year.

luck," and the word for fish, *yu (yü)*, is pronounced like the word for "surplus." Having these two dishes symbolizes that the family will have surplus fortune and luck in the New Year. In addition, the chicken is served whole with its head and feet, and the fish with its head and tail. This signifies that things will begin and end in proper ways in the New Year.

During the dinner, everybody repeatedly expresses good wishes for the New Year, and no unpleasant words may be spoken. If a child happens to break a bowl or plate—a common occurrence during the commotion of such a big meal—she or he is not to be scolded. Instead, people say to each other *"sui sui ping an,"* or "peace and safety every year" (the Chinese word for "broken," *sui*, is pronounced the same as the word for "year"). It is believed that the ill consequences of breaking something can be reversed with such an auspicious phrase.

After the dinner, the elder members of the family distribute *yasui qian (ya sui ch'ien)* to the children. *Yasui qian* means "money to

Chinese Zodiac Animals and the Qualities They Represent

Rat—(1984, 1996, 2008). Thrifty, well organized, charming.

Ox—(1985, 1997, 2009). Patient, stubborn, dependable.

Tiger—(1986, 1998, 2010). Brave, passionate, kind.

Rabbit—(1987, 1999, 2011). Neat and tidy, cautious, selfless.

Dragon—(1988, 2000, 2012). Full of vitality and strength, lucky, imaginative.

Snake—(1989, 2001, 2013). Deep thinker, mysterious, quiet.

Horse—(1990, 2002, 2014). Cheerful, talkative, quick-witted.

Sheep—(1991, 2003, 2015). Gentle and loving, compassionate, a strong believer.

Monkey—(1992, 2004, 2016). Smart, mischievous, an inventor.

Rooster—(1993, 2005, 2017). Confident, sharp, a perfectionist.

Dog—(1994, 2006, 2018). Loyal, trustworthy, alert.

Pig—(1995, 2007, 2019). Good natured, studious, reliable.

keep for the year." It is believed that giving children *yasui qian* can suppress evil and drive away demons, and with *yasui qian*, children can grow up healthy. In old times, *yasui qian* was usually 100 copper coins strung on red twine. Today it takes the form of paper money sealed in red envelopes called *hongbao*. Children usually get the biggest allowances of the year from these *hongbao*, and they can't be any happier.

Sleep is discouraged on New Year's Eve. There is an age-old tradition of staying up all night for the New Year. In the past, red candles were lit in every room of the house after the Happy Family Reunion Dinner; the light and color were supposed to make the most tenacious ghosts disappear. Family members sat together, eating fruit and snacks, playing games, or gambling until late at night or early in the morning. This tradition is called *shousui (shou sui)*, the New Year's Eve Vigil. *Shousui* signifies ringing out the old year and ringing in the new. It also expresses wishes for the longevity of parents. Today, few people stay up all night, but they typically wait until after midnight before retiring. Many families pass the hours by watching Spring Festival performances on the China Central Television network. As the clock ticks toward 12 o'clock, fireworks are set off at every household, producing deafening noise and thick smoke. As the New Year turns its page, people greet one another with "*xinnian kuaile*" ("*hsin nien k'uai lo*") or "*gonghe xinxi*" ("*kung ho hsin hsi*"), both meaning "Happy New Year." In the southern Chinese province of Guangdong, people often say "*gongxi facai*" ("*kung hsi fa ts'ai*"), meaning "good fortunes to you."

Chinese Zodiac

The Spring Festival is closely associated with the Chinese zodiac. The Chinese zodiac consists of 12 parts and is used as a 12-year calendar. Five cycles of the zodiac make up one complete cycle of 60 years, which is the basis of the Chinese calendar. In fact, there is no concept of century or millennium in the Chinese lunar calendar. Time proceeds in cycles of 60 years.

Each of the 12 years in the Chinese zodiac is ruled by one animal. The rat is the first, followed by the ox, tiger, rabbit, dragon, snake, horse, sheep, monkey, rooster, dog, and pig, in that order. Various legends account for the origin of the Chinese zodiac and the reason for such an order. One of them concerns the Buddha. Before he departed from earth, the Enlightened One invited all animals to a gathering by a large river in order to pick 12 of them to go with him. The Buddha set for the animals a contest: the first 12 that reached the other side of the river would be the winners. The rat, the most cunning of all, rode on the back of the ox and jumped off in front of the ox when they approached the other side of the river. Thus he became the first animal on the zodiac, and the ox the second. The lazy pig, as one can imagine, got the last place.

The Chinese believe that each person has personality traits that are similar to those of his or her zodiac animal. Traditional Chinese fortune-telling is very much based on the zodiac animals as well as the month, the day, and the hour of a person's birth. Each zodiac year holds different prospects for people according to their birth-year zodiac. During the Spring Festival, imagining what the zodiac animal in charge has in store for the coming year is a fun pastime for everybody. As China is a dragon-worshipping culture, people believe that those born in the Year of the Dragon are the luckiest, and the Year of the Dragon is also a year of good luck. Many folk beliefs are associated with the zodiac. For example, zodiac animals can affect marriages: a marriage between a "tiger girl" and a "rabbit man" is likely to run into trouble because the strengths of the partners are too unequally distributed. Another common belief is that when the zodiac year corresponds to one's birth zodiac (which means when one is 12, 24, 36, 48, 60, or 72 years old), it is a year of bad luck. Wearing a red band around the waist or a red string

RAT OX TIGER RABBIT

DRAGON SNAKE HORSE SHEEP

MONKEY ROOSTER DOG PIG

Symbols representing the 12 years of the Chinese zodiac.

around the neck is believed to be an effective way to counteract the ill fortune in this year.

In the New Year

New Year's Day is a day of relaxation for the Chinese. Enough food has been prepared beforehand, so even the busy housewives can sit back and enjoy the festivities with the rest of the family. As a custom, children wear brand-new clothes on New Year's Day. They run around happily in the neighborhood with candy and snacks. Adults mostly stay home, playing games, eating, and drinking.

There are a lot of taboos during the Spring Festival. On New

Year's Day, use of sharp instruments such as knives, scissors, or needles is forbidden because they would cut the good luck of the family. Brooms are also put away because if people were to sweep the ground, good luck and fortune would be swept away too. In old times, women would not leave the house on this day; if they did, good luck would also leave. If a person sleeps late in the morning, he or she is not to be woken up.

The next few days in the New Year are spent visiting relatives and friends and exchanging good wishes. Visitors usually bring gifts as well, as it is not considered polite to arrive empty-handed. This custom is called *bainian (pai nien)*. Everywhere people bow and

Workers in Shanghai remove a Spring Festival decoration in the shape of the *fu* character, which signifies fortune or blessings. The color red is commonly seen during the Spring Festival, as it represents good luck.

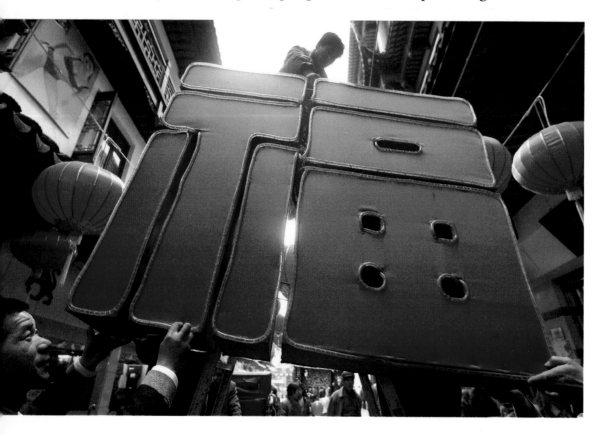

A man lights fireworks during a Spring Festival celebration in Taijing, in China's southwest Guizhou Province.

greet one another with *"gonghe xinxi," "gongxi facai,"* or other auspicious expressions. People prepare fruits, snacks, and big meals to treat their visitors. Children are probably the happiest of all during this time. They get more *yasui qian* from elder relatives when they pay the *bainian* visits, they can eat as much candy as they like, and they can pop firecrackers all the time.

Public performances are also popular during the Spring Festival. One of the most exciting events is the lion dance, a tradition that goes back hundreds of years. From the 4th to the 15th day of the New Year, lion dance groups tour from village to village, or from street to street in the cities. The performers wear shirts, pants, shoes, and headgear unique to their group.

The lion dance is not a dance with real lions. Rather, people use "dummy" lions to imitate the movements of the real animal. The dummy lion in these dances is often a wonderful piece of art. Its head is made of paper, cloth, or silk. It has big eyes that can open and close, a nose, and an open mouth. The cloth body, which features colorful

Auspicious Foods at the Spring Festival

Food	What It Represents
Fish	Surplus fortune and luck
Chicken	Good luck
Lamb or mutton	Good luck and family harmony
Noodles	Long life
Dumplings *(jiaozi)*	Fortune and good luck
Sweet rice cake *(niangao)*	Promotion step-by-step
Sweet rice balls	Family harmony
Tangerines and oranges	Good luck
Dates	Early spring

patterns that are drawn or embroidered, is often decorated with beautiful yellow tassels.

To do the lion dance, two performers go under the cover of the dummy lion, one holding the head and the other hunched over at the tail. The dancers wear shirts and pants that match the look of the lion. To the accompaniment of drums and gongs, they make all kinds of movements to imitate a lion in action: jumping, twisting, turning, pouncing, and so on. By long tradition, the spectators feed *hongbao* (money in red envelopes) into the mouth of the lion as a sign of inviting good luck. The skillful dancer holding the head takes the money as if the lion were eating it.

With the spread of Chinese culture, traditions like lion dances have also entered different countries. Today, in the large Chinese communities abroad, such as those in Hawaii, San Francisco, and New York City, lion dances are a frequent scene along store-lined streets during the Spring Festival.

The Lantern Festival

The official ending of the Spring Festival celebrations is *Deng Jie (Teng Chieh)*, the Lantern Festival. This festival is celebrated on the 15th day of the first lunar month and is also called *Yuanxiao (Yüan Hsiao)*, meaning "the evening with the first full moon."

The Lantern Festival, as its name suggests, is a feast of lanterns. It is believed to have started during the Han dynasty more than 2,000 years ago. According to one legend, the custom of hanging lanterns on Yuanxiao grew out of the ancient Chinese worship of the stars. The early Chinese believed that every star that shone in the sky represented one human being on earth. They regarded the stars as deities that brought them happiness and protected them from disasters and evils, and they put up beautiful lanterns to show their respect for the stars.

The display of elaborate lanterns is the major event of Yuanxiao. Every household hangs lanterns on the doors of the family home

Spectators feed *hongbao* into the mouth of the lion during a lion dance. This is a way to invite good luck.

and sets lanterns afloat on lakes and rivers. The traditional belief is that these lanterns will light the way of wandering ghosts to judgment and rebirth (in China belief in reincarnation is widespread). The night of the Lantern Festival is dreamlike: streets and houses are lit with lanterns of all shapes and colors. Lantern fairs are often held in public gardens or parks.

In old times, the lanterns were handcrafted from wood, bamboo, paper, silk, glass, or sometimes even thin pieces of jade. They were adorned with beautiful landscapes, human figures, flowers or fruits, or various animals. The human figures were often characters from folk stories. Flower and fruit lanterns included water lily, grape, melon, lotus, peony, and tangerine—all of which have auspicious meanings in Chinese culture. The animal lanterns featured

People walk past lanterns and a papier-mâché replica of the Temple of Heaven in a park in Beijing during celebration of the Lantern Festival. This event marks the last day of the Spring Festival.

the dragon, carp, horse, monkey, phoenix, and goldfish. In order to make the lantern show more exciting, people wrote riddles on their lanterns. Viewers competed with one another in solving these riddles, and the winner often took home the beautiful lantern as a prize.

Today, ready-made lanterns are mass-produced, and lightbulbs have replaced candles, but the old tradition of displaying lanterns and solving lantern riddles endures. Lantern fairs are held in various big cities on Yuanxiao. In the northern city of Harbin, an annual ice-lantern fair features beautiful lanterns carved from large blocks of river ice and illuminated with colorful neon lights. Each year it attracts thousands of visitors from all over the country, along with a growing number of tourists from foreign lands.

In the past, the Lantern Festival was also a time for boys and girls to get together, and it was a romantic night for young lovers. This is because unmarried Chinese women were generally not allowed to go out of the house during the year, and the night of the Lantern Festival was one of the few exceptions.

The characteristic food for the Lantern Festival is a sweet rice ball. In the North it is called *yuanxiao*, like the festival itself; in the South it is known as *tangyuan (t'ang yüan)*, meaning "round balls floating in the soup." The stuffing of *yuanxiao* is typically sweet, made from red bean paste, sweet crushed sesame seeds, or peanut paste, but in the South people also make savory *tangyuan* with meat and vegetable fillings. Because of its round shape, *yuanxiao* represents the full moon in the sky on the Lantern Festival night, and it is symbolic of family reunion, affection, and happiness.

Dragon boat racers line up before the start of a race in Hong Kong Harbor. The races are held every June to remember a famous Chinese poet and hero named Qu Yuan, who drowned himself out of love for his country.

4

The Dragon Boat Festival

The Dragon Boat Festival, the second of the three Chinese "festivals of the living," is celebrated on the fifth day of the fifth lunar month (hence it is also known as the "Double Fifth"). The festival corresponds to the period around the summer solstice (about June 21 on the Western calendar), when the sun reaches its highest point in the sky and the Northern Hemisphere experiences the most hours of daylight. To the Chinese, the Dragon Boat Festival is commonly known as *Duanwu Jie (Tuan Wu Chieh)*, the festival that celebrates the arrival of the fifth month.

The fifth lunar month brings tormenting heat and frequent heavy rain. Why is the arrival of such a month worth celebrating? The answer to this, to a certain extent, lies in the eternal dualism of Chinese philosophy. The Chinese have traditionally divided the world

A colorful dragon painted onto the door of a Chinese home. The dragon of Chinese mythology is much different from the dragons depicted in Western stories; the Chinese believe that although dragons are incredibly powerful, they are also benevolent as long as the proper sacrifices are observed.

into two principles: yin and yang. Yin, as the female element, is represented by women, water, darkness, night, and the moon; yang, the male element, is represented by men, fire, light, day, and the sun. Although yin and yang are forever in conflict, they are embedded in each other, and they alternate to bring balance and harmony into the world. The fifth month is the peak of the summer season, the midpoint of the year, and a dividing line between the yin and yang forces in nature. Before this month, the world is full of the growth and ripening that characterize the yang; after it the yang forces in nature start to decline, yielding to the dark and cold yin forces. In this sense, the fifth month is a representation of the Chinese belief that too great strength or too much power in itself bears the roots of decay and reversal, and people celebrate the fifth month as an important transitional point in nature.

Historians would add that the Dragon Boat Festival originated as a celebration of the fertility of the fields and the growth of rice. The transplanting of rice, a staple food that the Chinese have cultivated for thousands of years, is usually complete by the fifth lunar month. To ensure the healthy growth of the rice seedlings, people in ancient times offered sacrifices to the dragons—the guardians of rain in Chinese mythology—so they would give strength to the seedlings and protect them from harm.

Legendary History

If one were to ask ordinary Chinese people why they celebrate the Dragon Boat Festival, however, everybody would answer that it is to commemorate Qu Yuan (Ch'ü Yüan), the greatest poet in early classic Chinese literature. Qu Yuan lived in the third century B.C., a time when China was divided into a number of small kingdoms that constantly fought one another for control. This was the period in Chinese history known as the Warring States. A member of one of the highest native families in the Chu (Ch'u) kingdom of the South, Qu Yuan was minister and councilor to the king as well as a court poet of great fame. When his country was threatened by the growing power of the Qin (Ch'in) kingdom, Qu Yuan proposed domestic political reforms and the establishment of a legal system. However, his advice was rejected by the king, who was under the influence of a corrupt court. As a punishment, Qu Yuan was dismissed from his post and sent into exile. In 278 B.C., Qin soldiers stormed the capital of Chu, and the downfall of the state appeared imminent. In despair Qu Yuan, on the fifth day of the fifth lunar month, threw himself into the Miluo (Mi-lo) River, choosing death over seeing his country vanquished by the enemy.

When the fishermen in the area learned the news, they rushed to their boats and raced to rescue this beloved patriot and poet. Despite their efforts, Qu Yuan's body was never found. As a last resort, the fishermen threw rice into the water to feed the fish, shrimp, tortoises, and dragons so that they wouldn't eat Qu Yuan's body. The tradition of dragon boat races is said to have originated from the fishermen's race to rescue Qu Yuan.

Dragon Boat Races

Like the dragon in Western folklore, the Chinese dragon is a purely mythical creature. A marvelous mix of various earthly animals, it looks rather different from its Western counterpart. The Chinese dragon has the head of a camel, horns of a deer, eyes of a rabbit, ears of an ox, neck of a snake, belly of a frog, scales of a carp, claws of a hawk, and paws of a tiger. It has long whiskers and big shining pearls in its mouth. Unlike the Western dragon, which is often an evil force slain by human heroes, the Chinese dragon has a benevolent nature. It is the most powerful animal in Chinese mythology and has enjoyed an unsurpassed status in the Chinese culture. For centuries, kings and emperors believed they were the embodied dragons sent by heaven to rule the earth, and today Chinese people all over the world identify themselves as the "descendants of the dragons."

In Chinese mythology, dragons live in the water or in the clouds, so they are believed to be responsible for sending the spring rain, which is of great importance for a land with a long agricultural history. Dutiful dragons bring the right amounts of rainfall at the right time to guarantee a good harvest, while negligent ones cause flooding or drought. In old times, when floods or droughts did occur, people would make sacrifices to the dragons. These sacrifices frequently included animals, and sometimes even human beings. The dragon boat races are one example of the sacrifices to the dragons.

On the day of the Dragon Boat Festival, huge boats from nearby areas gather on lakes and rivers in central and southern China. These canoe-shaped boats, ranging from 40 to 100 feet in length, are built and decorated to look like dragons. They have an open-mouthed dragon head at the bow; a scaly body in the middle, and an upward-pointing tail at the stern, adding up to a vigorous-looking dragon in action. For speed in the water, the boats are constructed of light wood. Traditionally, the dragon boats come from different villages or clans. The crew typically consists of a group of rowers, a man waving flags at the bow, and a drum player at the stern. The flag waver and the drum player coordinate the rowers' motions.

Hundreds of people dressed in their holiday best swarm along riverbanks to watch the races. When the starting shot is fired, the colorful boats dart forth at full speed. The flag waver shouts orders at the top of his lungs, and the drum player beats a steady rhythm, producing sounds that can be heard miles away. The deafening noise of the races mimics the thunderous fights of the dragons in

Dragon boat racing is physically demanding, but victory generally brings a cash prize as well as the admiration of the assembled spectators.

Dragon boat races are held all over the world; these people are watching a race in New York City.

the sky, which, in Chinese folk belief, are the cause of rain. To intensify the competition, live targets such as ducks tied with colorful ribbons are often thrown into the river when the teams approach the finish line. The winning boat must capture one of the elusive waterfowl and cross the finish line ahead of the competition. Winners take home a cash prize, as well as the admiration of the spectators. Many boat teams practice all year long for this annual race, and they spare no effort to become the winner.

In the intense competition, it is not uncommon for the narrow boats to capsize. Sometimes members of a boat crew even drown. In the past, it was believed that a death or two at the dragon boat races was the rightful claim of the dragons—and nobody would even attempt to rescue a drowning rower.

Today dragon boat races are held not only in China but also in many areas that have large ethnic Chinese populations, including Southeast Asia and even North America. Since 1976 the annual World Championship International Dragon Boat Races have been held in Hong Kong Harbor, drawing in excess of 100 teams from more than 20 countries. Similar races, although smaller in scale, are held in the San Francisco Bay area and in Toronto, Canada, during the Dragon Boat Festival. Travelers flock to these places around the summer solstice to experience this spectacular event.

Festival Food

Zongzi (tsung tzu), the traditional food found in every Chinese home during the Dragon Boat Festival, is a tasty, glutinous rice dumpling wrapped in leaves. The origins of *zongzi* may be traced to the fishermen's attempts to keep water creatures from eating the body of Qu Yuan by throwing rice into the river. However, the transformation of rice into the rice dumpling didn't happen until much later. According to the legend, during the Eastern Han dynasty (A.D. 25–220), a fisherman happened to see the soul of Qu Yuan wandering along the river where he had drowned himself several hundred years earlier. The poet looked very sad and emaciated. He told the fisherman that he was grateful for people's rice offerings, but he was still starving because the dragons in the water had eaten all the rice. If people would wrap rice in small pieces of silk and bind the package with colorful threads, said the poet, the dragons wouldn't dare touch it. Apparently, the Chinese dragons, for some strange reason, were afraid of silk and colorful threads. After people did what Qu Yuan said, the wandering soul of the poet was never seen again, and people knew it was finally at peace (the Chinese have always believed that the dead need food as much as the living and that their souls will not rest unless they are properly fed). From then on, people kept the tradition of wrapping up the rice and eating the dumplings in memory of Qu Yuan.

In modern times, *zongzi* is no longer wrapped in silk, but usually in bamboo, lotus, or reed leaves. These leaves, when cooked, give the rice a very peculiar fragrance. *Zongzi* varies in shape and ingredients from area to area. The dumplings may come in triangles, cones, or cylinders. Some are made of pure glutinous rice and eaten with honey or sugar; some have sweet stuffing, like bean paste, date paste, sesame, or assortments of nuts; and others have savory fillings like pork, ham, sausage, shrimp, and mushrooms. *Zongzi* may take hours to cook—only by simmering for a long time will the glutinous rice be soft enough and the fragrance of the wrapping leaves permeate the rice. In China almost every family has its own *zongzi* recipes, and presenting homemade *zongzi* as gifts to friends and relatives is a centuries-old custom. In some areas of China, salted duck eggs are eaten together with *zongzi*; in other areas, green bean cakes are favored. Today, ready-made *zongzi* are available everywhere during the Dragon Boat Festival. Even grocery stores in overseas Chinese communities carry these rice dumplings to give the Chinese abroad a taste of home.

The Poisonous Fifth Month

As noted earlier, the month during which the Dragon Boat Festival takes place is characterized by the struggle between the dual forces of yin and yang. The yang element, with all the growth in spring and early summer, has reached its peak by now, whereas the yin element, with the looming decay of autumn and winter, is about to gain the upper hand. The fifth lunar month is the hottest month of the year. With everything in full growth, various poisonous vermin also start to multiply. Evil vapors abound in the air, and all sorts of mischievous spirits are lurking around the corner, ready to attack. The fifth month is considered a dangerous month, and the Chinese used to call it the "poisonous month." In the ancient past, a child born on the fifth day of this month was not even allowed to live, for it was believed that the baby would bring great harm to the family.

The dragon boat races, as previously discussed, were both a commemoration of Qu Yuan and a ceremony for rain. But they had an additional function in the dangerous fifth month: repelling evil. The jollity and power demonstrated by the dragon boats during the races were intended to drive away demons. At the end of the races, crews would often cast offerings into the river as a symbol of washing pestilence downstream. However, for a time when danger lurked everywhere, dragon boat races alone were not believed to be quite enough.

Today, Chinese people continue to take extra precautions during the "poisonous fifth month." Visitors to a Chinese home—especially one in the countryside—during the Dragon Boat Festival will very likely see bunches of plants hanging from the door hinges. These are sweet flag and mugwort, two plants that have kept Chinese people safe through the dangerous month for centuries. The leaves of sweet flag are shaped like swords and are thus believed to have demon-slaying power. Women used to wear these leaves in their hair to keep away demons. Mugwort has a pungent scent and is often burned in the

The Chinese believe that drinking realgar wine can protect them against the "poisonous fifth month," which has long been considered a dangerous time when evil spirits are waiting to attack the unsuspecting.

FAST FACTS

The Dragon Boat Festival

Date:	5th day of the 5th lunar month
Also called:	Double Fifth or *Duanwu*
Festival food:	Rice dumplings, salted duck eggs, and green bean cakes
Activities:	Dragon boat races
Legendary figure:	Qu Yuan, a patriotic poet from 2,300 years ago

house for cleansing purposes; its odor is believed to have the ability to kill off pestilence. Garlic bunches are sometimes used together with the sweet flag and mugwort.

Extra insurance against the poison of this month comes from a wine with realgar (arsenic sulfide) in it. The Chinese have long found that realgar, like sweet flag and mugwort, can kill germs. They also believe that it is effective in keeping away poisonous creatures like scorpions and centipedes. During the Dragon Boat Festival, the wine was the staple drink, and parents used to smear it on their children's faces and bodies to keep them from harm. This close association with the Dragon Boat Festival stemmed from the belief that the wine was most effective on the Double Fifth day, when it could not only keep away pestilence but also turn a vermin in disguise back into its original form.

The famous Tale of a White Snake in Chinese folklore tells the story of how a happy union of a snake and a young scholar was torn apart by the magic power of the realgar wine. The white snake in the story yearned for love and family life in the human world. She went through great pains to transform herself into the form of a beautiful woman (Chinese people often compare a beautiful but dangerous woman to a snake and call her a "beauty snake"). At the lovely West Lake in eastern China, she met a young scholar. They fell in love and became man and wife. Just as they were at the point of "living happily ever after," a nosy and rather condemnable monk appeared. For some reason, he was upset about the fact that a snake could have a happy life like a human, so he told the innocent husband to serve his wife some realgar wine on the fifth day of the fifth month. After drinking the wine, the poor wife was turned back into a snake. The husband was frightened to death at the sight, and their love story was thus ended. This folktale frequently wins enormous sympathy for the snake, yet it is also a legendary proof of the evil-subduing power of the realgar wine.

"Five poison charms" are yet another way of keeping away the diseases and pestilence of the fifth month. The five poisons refer to toads, lizards, scorpions, snakes, and centipedes. Pictures of these poisonous creatures are posted on the doors of every household during this month. Often the pictures also contain a large cock that is busy killing the five poisons. Children wear small pieces of clothing with the five poisons motif, to keep away the vermin.

It was commonly believed that when put together in a closed container without food, the five poisons would kill each other off. The last one would take on the poison of the other four and become the most powerful. As Wolfram Eberhard relates in his book *Chinese Festivals*, an old folk belief attributed a peculiar magic property to the powder made from the dead and dried survivor: if dissolved in wine or put in food, the powder would make the person who ingested it fall in love with the person who served it.

A family looks at one of the dragon lanterns on display at Victoria Park in Hong Kong. The Mid-Autumn Festival, one of the most important Chinese festivals, is held during the eighth lunar month.

The Mid-Autumn Festival

When the eighth lunar month arrives, the Chinese are ready for another big festival. The 15th day of this month, which usually falls in mid- to late September on the Western calendar, is the last of the three "festivals of the living." Called *Zhongqiu Jie* (*Chung Ch'iu Chieh*), or the Mid-Autumn Festival, it is second only to the Chinese New Year in importance among all Chinese festivals. The Mid-Autumn Festival is so named because in the Chinese seasons, the seventh, eighth, and ninth lunar months constitute autumn, and the 15th day of the eighth month falls in the very middle.

The beginnings of the Mid-Autumn Festival can be traced back almost 2,500 years. The *Book of Rites*, written during the Zhou (Chou) dynasty, describes that the kings worshipped the sun in spring and the moon in autumn. Though it began as a festival of the harvest—as a time to celebrate, and thank the gods for, the blessings of a successful growing season, as well as to pray for a good harvest in the coming year—the Mid-Autumn Festival soon became a celebration of the moon and of family reunion. It may not be the most spectacular of Chinese festivals, but it is certainly the most romantic.

Customs

The Mid-Autumn Festival is also known as the Moon Festival, for the moon is the center of its celebrations. Because the Chinese calendar is based on the cycles of the moon, with each month starting on a new moon, there is always a full moon on the 15th of the month. On the evening of the Mid-Autumn Festival, the moon is at its lowest angle to the horizon, which makes it appear brighter and larger than at any other time of the year. In American lore, this is the Harvest Moon or Hunter's Moon. For the Chinese, it is the only time that the moon is perfectly round, making it an ideal symbol of family togetherness and harmony, among the most cherished values in the Chinese culture. On this day, people make every effort to join the family reunion, and even daughters-in-law who have gone to visit their own parents must return home (traditionally, a Chinese woman lives with her husband's family after marriage).

The Mid-Autumn Festival is a special occasion for the womenfolk. As an old Chinese saying goes, "Women do not worship the Kitchen God, and men do not worship the moon." Women are the center of this festival and are in charge of the sacrifices to the moon because in Chinese cosmology the moon represents the yin, or female element. The Mid-Autumn Festival is the time of year when the yin gains ascendancy in nature: the hot summer is going away and the cold winter is setting in. Because the full moon represents the fullness of the yin element, women—who represent the yin force in the world of humans—are put in charge of the festival.

Celebrations don't usually start until after nightfall. Customarily, an altar will be set up in the family courtyard to make sacrifices to the moon. Women prepare, and place on the altar, plates filled with round fruits such as apples, peaches, crab apples, watermelons, grapes, and pomegranates. The shape of these fruits symbolizes the fullness of the moon, which represents family unity and harmony. Peaches are also a symbol of longevity, while pomegranates and watermelons, with their numerous seeds, represent the Chinese ideal of many sons in the family. As on many other happy occasions, the pear—which in any case isn't round—is excluded, because the

The Mid-Autumn Festival began as a festival to give thanks for the harvest, but gradually it developed into a celebration of the moon. According to Chinese mythology, the moon is inhabited by the Jade Rabbit, who mixes the elixir of immortality. This Asian print shows the Jade Rabbit playing with a monkey who, according to another story, stole and ate peaches of longevity.

Chinese word for pear, *li*, is pronounced the same as the word for separation.

The festival's distinctive food, *yuebing (yüeh ping)*, or moon cake—so called because of its full-moon-like shape—is the highlight on the altar. Usually, 13 moon cakes, representing the number of months in

FAST FACTS

The Mid-Autumn Festival

Date:	15th day of the 8th lunar month
Also called:	The Moon Festival or Zhongqiu
Festival food:	Moon cakes and round fruits
Activities:	Moon gazing, family reunion, get-togethers with friends
Legendary figures:	Chang E, the Moon Goddess; the woodcutter Wu Gang; the matchmaker Yuexia Laoren

a complete Chinese year (that is, a leap year), are placed like a pyramid on the center of the altar to represent a full circle of happiness. (In contrast to Westerners, the Chinese don't regard 13 as an ominous number.) The moon cake is a sweet pastry made only at this time of the year. It varies in style from area to area despite a common name. There are two major styles of moon cakes. Those made in Suzhou in eastern China are like shortbread, with several layers containing gingko, bean paste, bacon, shrimp, fruits, or nuts. Those made in Guangzhou, or Canton, in South China have very thin dough and rich stuffing such as coconut paste, lotus seed paste, assorted fruits and nuts, and very often an egg yolk (which symbolizes the full moon). The Chinese characters for such auspicious words as "longevity," "fortune," and "happiness," or pictures representing traditional moon legends, are often molded on the top of the moon cakes.

Today, moon cakes are available not only in China, but also in Chinese communities overseas. Around the Mid-Autumn Festival,

Asian grocery stores everywhere display stacks of moon cakes for sale in beautifully ornamented packages, usually placed at the most prominent spot in the store. By modern standards, the moon cake would be considered unhealthy for its high cholesterol and fat content. Nonetheless, the sweet pastry has been the traditional food of the Mid-Autumn Festival for centuries and is always a favorite gift at this time of year.

Alongside the round fruits and moon cakes on the altar, there is often a clay statue or a picture of a Jade Rabbit. This rabbit, called Tu'er Ye (T'u Erh Yeh), is a favorite toy of children during the festival. Sometimes a picture of the Moon Goddess is also displayed. These two figures came from a famous moon legend, which will be discussed in depth later.

Moon cakes are eaten during the Mid-Autumn Festival.

Just at the hour when the moon clears the treetops and shines brightly over the earth, the moon worship begins. The women in the family go forward to the altar and bow to the moon one after another, while the men stay behind. After that, the women cut the moon cakes into slices; the number of slices should be the same as the number of all family members, including those who have been unable to make it home for the festivities. Then the social pleasures of the night begin. The whole family will sit in the courtyard, or sometimes a group of friends will go to the top of a tall building. They eat moon cakes and fruits, drink chrysanthemum wine, and play games late into the night.

Moon gazing is the highlight, as the moon is the theme of this special night. People praise the moon's luminous and gentle light and express their wishes for family prosperity and harmony. This is also a night for poets and writers, and some of the greatest Chinese literature was created under the full moon of mid-autumn. One of the best-known poems written on this occasion was composed in the year 1076 by Su Shi (Su Shih), who had been sent into exile by the emperor:

How many times has the moon shone full?

Lifting my cup I ask the blue sky.

In the palaces and towers of Heaven

What season is it tonight, I wonder.

I should like to ride there on the wind,

But I fear I could not stand the cold

Of those crystal domes and jade halls on high.

I rise and dance and make my shadow move:

How much nicer it is here!

Over vermilion chambers,

Through curtained windows

Shining on the sleepless—

The moon should not be blamed.

But why always full when friends are separated?

Men are happy or sad, apart or together,

The moon is obscured or clear, waxing or waning:

In this world perfection seldom comes.

I only hope that we can live long

And both enjoy the moon's beauty, though a thousand miles
apart.

**(Translated by James Robert Hightower, in *The Columbia Anthology
of Traditional Chinese Literature*, ed. Victor H. Mair.
New York: Columbia University Press, 1994.)**

Today, these verses are widely recited during the Mid-Autumn Festival, and not simply by people in China. Many people of Chinese ancestry living in other countries—even some whose families left China decades ago—continue to regard China as their homeland. For them the Mid-Autumn Festival is a special time of nostalgia for the Chinese culture, and Su Shi's words encapsulate their feelings.

While other members of the family are enjoying the festival feast, girls have an important piece of business to attend to: they retreat to a quiet place and send the moon their special wishes. Most of these wishes, as one might guess, have to do with love and marriage. From ancient times up until about 100 years ago, Chinese girls had no say in their own marriages, as parents and matchmakers typically chose a girl's husband. In fact, most girls didn't even meet their husbands until their wedding day. Because marriage decisions were out of their hands, girls regarded it as very important to pray to the Moon Goddess and the legendary matchmaker Yuexia Laoren (Yüeh Hsia Lao Jen), or the Old Man in the Moon, on this day of the full moon. These wishes, however, could not be spoken out loud, for to do so meant they would fail to come true.

Myths and Legends

Various moon myths and legends make the Mid-Autumn Festival fascinating. In the Chinese culture, the moon is the habitat of the immortals and has always been a heaven for those who hope to attain eternal life. The Chinese moon, as a matter of fact, has a very interesting population. It basically consists of a woman who flew to the moon thousands of years before Neil Armstrong, a woodcutter who is faced with a task as frustrating as that of Sisyphus, a rabbit who is constantly pounding the elixir of immortality, and an old man who takes care of all marital affairs on the earth.

The most popular figure on the moon is Chang E (Ch'ang O). This is the goddess to whom girls send their secret wishes on the mid-autumn night. Chang E lives in the "Palace of Great Cold" and has been a character in Chinese literature for thousands of years. Her story begins in remote antiquity when one day, 10 suns, which are supposed to take turns shining, rise in the sky at the same time. The earth is scorched and burnt. To save his people from a deadly fate, the great king Yao sends his master archer, Hou Yi (Hou I), to bring down these misbehaving suns. A man whose courage matches his great marksmanship, Hou Yi draws his bow and shoots down nine of the suns, leaving only one to carry out the duty of shining, and thus saving life on earth.

The Queen Mother of the West, who resides in the Kunlun (K'un-lun) Mountains somewhere in present-day Tibet, takes notice of Hou Yi's heroic deed and sends him the elixir of life as a reward. She tells him that he should not take it until he feels worthy enough to

An illustration of the mythical figure Chang E, who stole the elixir of life from her husband and flew to the moon.

become an immortal. Hou Yi, a very conscientious man, hides the elixir in his house and goes out to perform more good deeds to show his sincerity in cultivating immortality. While he is gone, his wife, Chang E, sees a glowing light coming from where Hou Yi has hidden the elixir. Curious, she finds the magic potion and swallows it. Immediately she becomes so light that she floats into the air. Her husband comes home just in time to see her flying away; it is too late to pull her back. Chang E flies all the way to the moon, where she finds herself alone in the Palace of Great Cold. She coughs up some of the magic potion, and it turns into a white rabbit.

From that day on, Chang E has been separated from her husband. They meet only once a year, on the mid-autumn day. The wife became the Moon Goddess, granting romantic wishes to those who pray to her, whereas the husband kept to his duty of guarding the sun. Meanwhile the little rabbit, fondly called the Jade Rabbit, became Chang E's only companion on the cold moon and has been pounding more elixir of immortality with a mortar ever since.

Another interesting resident of the moon is the woodcutter Wu Gang (Wu Kang). Whether he and Chang E know each other the legends never tell. While assigned to guard the making of the elixir of life during his studies to become an immortal, Wu Gang fell asleep. To punish him, the Jade Emperor sent Wu Gang to fell a big cassia tree on the moon. Unfortunately, every time Wu Gang completed an ax cut, the tree's wound miraculously healed. Thus the poor Chinese Sisyphus, suffering from perhaps the most severe penalty for dozing off during studying, has been chopping on the cassia tree for more than 2,000 years!

According to Chinese folklore, all earthly marriages are predetermined by Yuexia Laoren—the Old Man in the Moon—who is called Yuelao for short. This old graybeard, who enjoys playing chess with the God of Longevity, arranges people's marriages by tying a magic red string between the feet of the future man and wife when they are just newborns. Because of this string, the two will always find each other when they grow up, no matter how far away they might be. "Their marriage is drawn together across thousands of miles by the red string," Chinese people commonly say when a husband and wife come from places that are far away from each other. On the night of the Mid-Autumn Festival, girls pray to both Chang E and Yuelao (which is also a respectful name for a successful matchmaker) for their dream husbands.

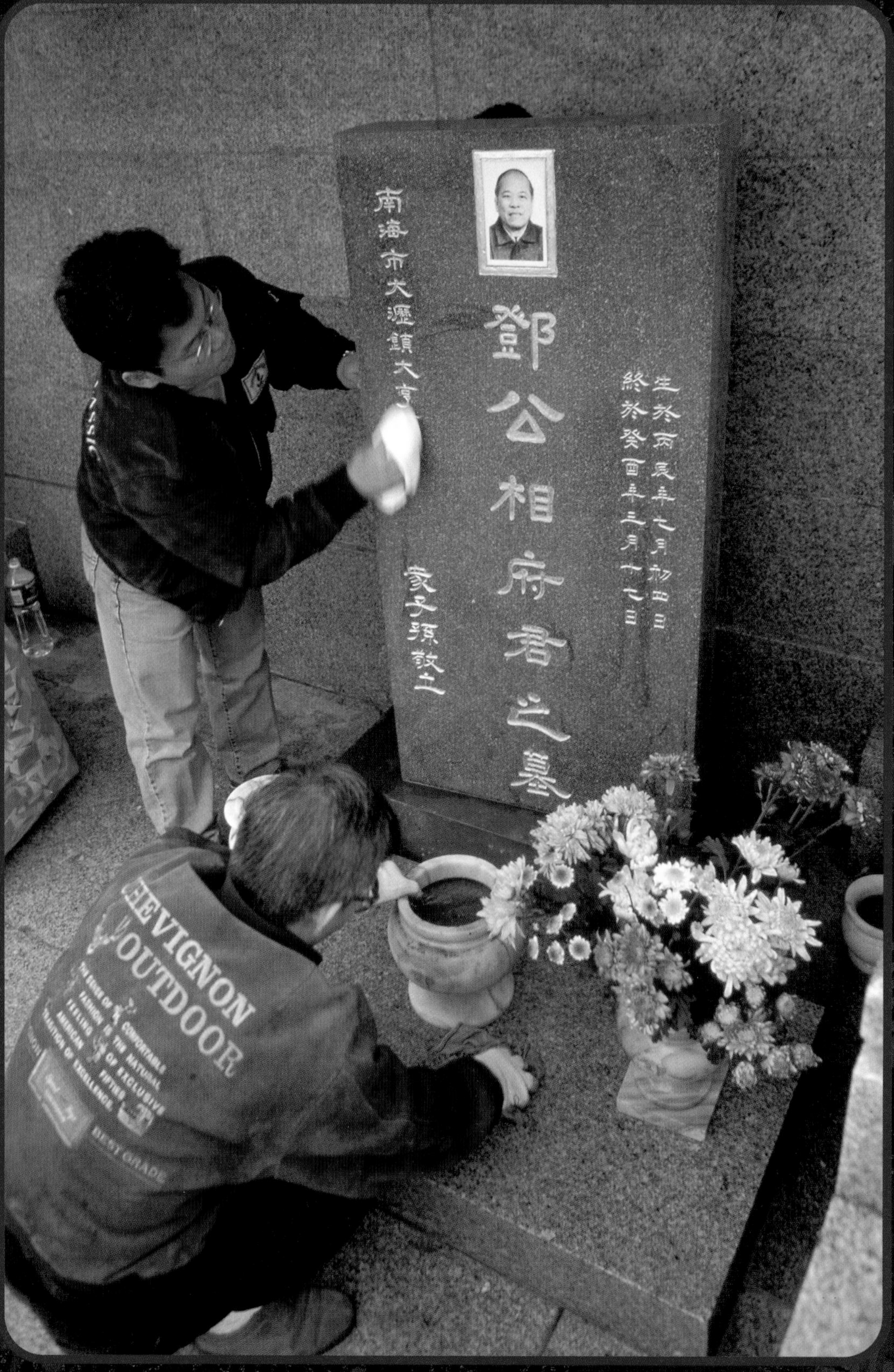
南海市大瀝鎮大
鄧公相府君之墓
HEVIGNON
OUTDOOR
BEST GRADE

Family members clean the grave of a loved one during the Qingming Festival. This observance, also known as the Clear Brightness, is an important "festival of the dead" celebrated in China.

6

Clear Brightness, the Ghost Festival, Qiqiao, and Chongyang

Every month on the Chinese calendar has national or local festivals and celebrations. In addition to the three "festivals of the living" discussed in previous chapters, there are four other significant festivals observed throughout the country. Two of the three traditional "festivals of the dead" are still widely celebrated today: *Qingming (Ch'ing Ming)*, the Clear Brightness; and *Zhongyuan Jie (Chung Yüan Chieh)*, the Ghost Festival. *Qiqiao (Ch'i Ch'iao)*, the Double Seventh, is dedicated to romantic love. *Chongyang (Ch'ung Yang)*, the Double Ninth, is a holiday for family survival and for elder people.

Clear Brightness

Many cultures celebrate the coming of spring. In China, Qingming (literally "Clear Brightness") is a festival marking the reappearance of warmth and the reawakening of nature.

Clear Brightness is a rarity among traditional Chinese festivals in that it falls on a fixed date on the Western calendar (April 4 or April 5). At this time of the year, the coldest of the winter is over, the air has become clear, the days are getting brighter, grass is turning green, and flowers are beginning to bloom. In the remote past, this festival was a holiday celebrated with dancing, singing, and picnicking. Over time, it gradually evolved into a day dedicated to the commemoration of ancestors.

The Clear Brightness Festival is also known as *Hanshi (Han Shih)*, or the Cold Food Festival. On this day, people eat only cold food. This tradition is in memory of a man named Jie Zitui (Chieh Tzu-t'ui), who lived about 2,600 years ago during the Spring and Autumn period. This was a time when, as in the Warring States period that followed, China consisted of a number of small states fighting one another for control of the whole nation. Jie Zitui was a loyal follower of a feudal lord named Chong'er (Ch'ung Erh), who at one time was forced to live in exile in a foreign land for 19 years. In the midst of the hardships of exile, most of Chong'er's followers left him; only Jie Zitui and a few others remained with their ruler. Once, during a period of desperate starvation, Jie Zitui cut off a piece of his own leg, served it to his lord, and saved Chong'er's life.

Later Chong'er returned to his state and became one of the most powerful lords of his time. He rewarded many of his faithful followers with titles and lands but somehow forgot about Jie Zitui. When he finally thought of Jie Zitui one day, he discovered that his loyal servant had long left and become a hermit in the remote mountains. Chong'er dispatched emissaries to retrieve Jie Zitui, but despite many offers of gifts, the hermit refused to return. Finally, Chong'er had his men set fire to the mountains where Jie Zitui was living, hoping that this would smoke out his once loyal servant. After the fire had died down, however, Jie Zitui was found burnt to death, his hands still clinging to a scorched willow tree. A poem left by the hermit explained that he would rather die than compromise his integrity for riches, and that his only wish was for his lord to be a wise ruler. People were deeply moved by Jie Zitui's integrity. To commemorate his great spirit, they decided to set aside the day as a time when no fire would be allowed. Because Jie Zitui died on the day of Clear Brightness, it has since become a tradition to eat only cold food on this day.

On the Clear Brightness, the whole family goes to visit the ancestral graves. They sweep the gravestones, clear weeds, and tidy up the gravesides. They also bring offerings of cold food, pastries, and fresh fruit for their ancestors to "enjoy." In addition, they make

A couple burns paper money, thereby sending it to the spirit of an ancestor, in front of a grave at a public cemetery in Shanghai.

paper spirit money and burn it in front of the graves as a way of transmitting it to the ancestors in the underworld. In some areas people leave some spirit money on the top of the tombs after the ceremony, to indicate that the graves are still being cared for. In other areas a bamboo pole with a paper ribbon tied on the top serves the same purpose.

The Chinese believe that their ancestors exert strong influences on their everyday life. The ancestors had laid the foundation for the family during the course of their lives, and after death they still play important roles in the family. If they are well cared for, they will bless the family with prosperity and many offspring. If they are not, the family is unlikely to thrive. As a result, visiting the family graves and caring for the ancestors become important duties for all living members of the family. On the Clear Brightness, even those who cannot make it home will prepare offerings from afar in the hope that their "sacrifice from a distance" will reach their ancestors at home. Today, Chinese people all over the world still observe the tradition of *saomu (sao mu)*, or "sweeping the graves," on the Clear Brightness by visiting their family graveyard and offering their ancestors food, incense, and spirit money.

However, the Clear Brightness is not a day to mourn. Crying at the graves is forbidden by tradition. This is a day to honor ancestors, but it is also a time for the living to enjoy. After the sacrifice, food offerings will be removed and taken aside for a picnic by the family, as is appropriate for the Cold Food Festival.

The Clear Brightness is also a day when the family makes the first excursion of the year in the fields. In old times, residents in urban areas would dress up and go into the countryside to enjoy the warm spring weather and the green vegetation. This is known as *taqing (t'a ch'ing)*, or "treading on the green." It was also a time for girls and boys to play and to court each other. Today, playing on swings remains a popular activity during this festival. As a tradition, people hang willow branches above their doors, and women wear willow twigs in their hair to keep away evil spirits.

But the favorite pastime during the Clear Brightness is probably kite flying. Kites originated in China more than 2,000 years ago and at one time had a practical function: armies used them to send messages. Today, however, kites are merely a popular folk craft. Chinese kites come in various shapes and forms: swallows, butter-flies, carp, crabs, dragonflies, and even legendary animals such as phoenixes and dragons. At this time of the year, the winds are

A young woman flies a kite on the Great Wall. Kite flying is a popular pastime that originated in China more than 2,000 years ago.

always favorable for kite flying. In the open fields, people fly their kites, vying to get them as high as possible. If a kite happens to break away from the string and disappears, it means bad luck is also gone. One should not pick up a lost kite, as it is equivalent to picking up bad luck from others.

The Ghost Festival

The second "festival of the dead" comes on the 15th day of the seventh lunar month and is called Zhongyuan Jie (literally, "the Middle of the Year Festival"). Because of its special ceremonies, however, it is more commonly known as *Gui Jie (Kuei Chieh)*, or "the Ghost Festival."

For the Chinese, the seventh lunar month is the "month of ghosts." At this time of the year, all ghosts are released from the confines of the underworld. They return to, and wander freely in, the world above, exerting a strong influence on the living. The Ghost Festival, celebrated in the middle of the seventh month, has both a Taoist and a Buddhist background. Taoists believe that this is the day when the envoy of the underworld comes above to judge the behavior of both humans and ghosts. He punishes or rewards each according to the sins committed or the good deeds performed. Buddhists, on the other hand, believe that this is a day to feed the hungry ghosts and to help their souls get released from purgatory. In both cases ghosts, rather than humans, are the reason for the festival.

While the Clear Brightness is to honor the family ghosts, the Ghost Festival is mainly for the ghosts of strangers and the uncared-for dead. According to traditional Chinese beliefs, after people die, their souls go to live in the zones of formlessness until the time for their rebirth comes. If these souls have descendants to care for them and make offerings from time to time, they lead a comfortable "life" in the underworld. The souls of those who died without children, or who died a bad death (from murder, drowning, execution for a crime, or suicide, for example), suffer from want of food and insatiable desires. In such cases, these hungry, desperate ghosts come up to the human world during the month of ghosts, seeking not only to exact revenge but also to find a replacement. Only by finding someone to replace them in the underworld can such souls free themselves from want and be reborn.

Thus, during the seventh lunar month, people need to be very careful so as not to become a replacement for a hungry ghost. They use extra caution in potentially dangerous activities such as swimming, for hungry ghosts are lurking everywhere. Some people turn to Buddhist monks and Taoist priests, who perform rituals at temples or monasteries to keep them safe. These monks and priests chant scriptures and offer food, incense, paper clothes, and spirit money to the dead. In such ceremonies, all

Women present offerings of food, money, and incense during the Ghost Festival. Chinese Buddhists believe that this is a day to feed hungry ghosts and help their spirits win release from purgatory.

souls are invited to come and enjoy the meal prepared for them so they will no longer suffer from hunger, thirst, or unfulfilled desires. These souls are also asked to give up any malevolent intent and watch over and help the living. At home, people make sacrifices to these uncared-for and hungry ghosts in a similar fashion.

On the night of the Ghost Festival, lion dances and various acrobatic shows are performed. Lanterns are also hung in front of houses to light the way so that the wandering ghosts can find their homes. A very special ceremony performed on the night of the Ghost Festival is called *fang hedeng (fang ho teng)*, or "floating the river lanterns." Every family makes candlelit lanterns and sets them afloat on a river. Most of these lanterns are in the shape of a lotus flower, as in Buddhism the lotus flower symbolizes the release of the soul from purgatory. It is believed that these lanterns can illuminate the way out for ghosts and spirits in the underworld. When a lantern sinks into the water, it means that it has been picked up by a hungry ghost, who will then be reborn. If in the late night there are still lanterns floating on the water, people take it to mean that there are no more hungry ghosts around.

Qiqiao

During the same month when the ghosts wander freely in the human world, there is a day dedicated to romantic love. This is the seventh day of the seventh lunar month, which is considered an especially lucky time for women, as it is the day when the fairies travel around. Romance fills the air as one of the most famous couples in Chinese folklore, the Cowherd and the Weaving Maid, cross the Heavenly River for their annual reunion in the starry sky. This is the festival of Qiqiao, or the "Double Seventh."

An early legend of Qiqiao says that the Weaving Maid was a daughter of the Emperor of Heaven. She lived at the eastern bank

FAST FACTS

Three Festivals of the Dead

Qingming, the Clear Brightness

Date:	April 4 or 5
Activities:	"Sweeping the graves" of the family ancestors and eating cold foods.

Ghost Festival

Date:	15th day of the 7th lunar month
Activities:	Lighting the way for the wandering ghosts to go home and find their rebirth.

Sending the Winter Clothes

Date:	1st day of the 10th lunar month
Activities:	Burning paper clothes to ancestors to keep them warm during the cold winter.

of the Heavenly River and weaved all day long to make beautiful garments. She worked so hard that she didn't even have time to take care of her appearance. The Emperor of Heaven, seeing that his daughter was single and lonely, married her to the Cowherd at the western bank of the Heavenly River. The happy couple, however, fell so in love with each other that they completely forgot about their duties: the bride stopped weaving, and the groom no longer tended his cattle. When the Emperor of Heaven learned this, he became very angry. He ordered the Weaving Maid to return to the eastern bank of the river, and the Cowherd to the western bank, to resume their respective duties. However, as he was not without sympathy, he allowed the two to meet once a year on the seventh night of the seventh month.

A more popular version of the story of Qiqiao begins with the Cowherd, an honest and hardworking young orphan whose only companion was an old ox left by his parents. The two, who were like brothers, depended on each other for a living. When the Cowherd grew up, the ox felt sorry that he was single and promised to help him find a wife. He told the Cowherd that on a particular day of a particular month, the seven daughters of the Emperor of Heaven would come down to the earth to play and bathe in a nearby river. If the Cowherd hid the clothes of one of the girls, she would fall in love with him and marry him. On that particular day, the Cowherd, following the ox's advice, successfully brought home the Weaving Maid, the youngest daughter of the Emperor of Heaven. The two fell deeply in love, and the Weaving Maid decided not to return to heaven anymore. They became man and wife and lived happily together.

When the Emperor of Heaven found out that his beloved daughter had married the Cowherd and given up her life in heaven, he was very upset and sent the Queen Mother of the West to bring her back. As the Queen Mother was taking away the Weaving Maid, the old ox of the Cowherd turned his horn into a boat for his master to ride and follow his wife. However, just when the Cowherd was about to reach the Weaving Maid, the Queen Mother pulled a silver pin from her hair and drew with it a Heavenly River across the sky, which forever separated the husband and wife. The sad fate of these two star-crossed lovers deeply touched the phoenix, king of all birds. He called all magpies together to form a bridge over the Heavenly River on the seventh day of the seventh month so that the Weaving Maid and the Cowherd could cross the river and reunite on this night.

If the sky is clear on the night of the Double Seventh, one can see the star of the Cowherd (Altair) and the star of the Weaving Maid (Vega) close to each other by the misty Milky Way. This is their night of reunion across the bridge spanned by the magpies over the Heavenly River. Thick clouds often cover the happy meeting of the two, and any rain that falls during the night is said to be the tears of the parting couple. In real life, Altair and Vega are 16 light-years apart, yet it is a universal belief that love transcends distance and physical presence, as was expressed in this famous poem by Qin Guan (Ch'in Kuan) from the Song (Sung) dynasty:

Among the beautiful clouds,

Over the heavenly river,

Crosses the weaving maiden.

A night of rendezvous,

Across the autumn sky,

Surpasses joy on earth.

Moments of tender love and dream,

So sad to leave the magpie bridge.

Eternal love between us two,

Shall withstand the time apart.

(Translated by Kylie Hsu, at
http://www.calstatela.edu/faculty/khsu2/poetry3.html/)

The Weaving Maid is traditionally regarded as a patron spirit for women's work, and like the Mid-Autumn Festival, Qiqiao is mainly

Chinese couples celebrate after a mass wedding in Shanghai. The Chinese, superstitious about the importance of numbers, consider nine an auspicious number that signifies good luck and happiness. Because of this, many Chinese wanted to be married on September 9, 1999, an especially lucky day.

a women's celebration. It is often called *Nü'er Jie (Nü Erh Chieh)*, "the Maiden's Day," or "the Daughter's Day." On the day of Qiqiao, girls make offerings to the Weaving Maid and pray for a pair of nimble hands and cleverness. The name of the festival, Qiqiao, is also the name for this special ceremony.

Traditional offerings on Qiqiao, not surprisingly, consisted mainly of objects associated with girls and women, such as needles, combs, mirrors, and flowers. In the past, contests were held to see which girl could thread a special needle with seven holes the fastest. The winner was considered the cleverest and the best at needlework.

Another traditional activity of Qiqiao involved spiders. Girls put a spider into their jewelry box on the night before Qiqiao. If the spider had made a strong and well-knit web by the next morning, this indicated that the Weaving Maid would grant the wishes of the jewelry box's owner.

Today, many of these traditional activities are no longer observed. Still, Qiqiao remains a festival for romance and love, functioning somewhat like a Chinese Valentine's Day.

Chongyang

Autumn is a beautiful season. Leaves are turning gold, the sky is high and blue, and the air is crisp and clear. It's a good time for mountain climbing and other outings to enjoy nature, and one of the traditional Chinese festivals is dedicated to such activities. This is Chongyang, or the "Double Ninth"—so called because it is the ninth day of the ninth month. The yin-yang dualism in the Chinese culture extends to numbers: even numbers are regarded as yin (negative and female) and odd numbers as yang (positive and male). The number nine, as the largest of the yang numbers, is considered the most auspicious of all numbers. It signifies good luck, happiness, and longevity and is widely used in many aspects of Chinese life. For example, in the Ming and Qing dynasties, the imperial palace had 9,999 rooms, and on September 9, 1999, mass weddings were held all over China.

The festival of Chongyang was being celebrated as early as the Eastern Han dynasty, about 2,000 years ago. Legend has it that a famous Taoist priest called Fei Changfang (Fei Ch'ang-fang) once warned a diligent disciple of his, Huan Jing (Huan Ching), that a plague was going to befall his village on a particular day. The priest told Huan Jing that to escape the disaster, the villagers had to wear pouches filled with cornel leaves, drink chrysanthemum wine, and go up to a mountain. When the day came, Huan Jing and the people of his village did what they were told. When they came back home from the mountains, they found all their livestock dead from the plague. Grateful to Fei Changfang, and happy to have survived the disaster, people set aside the day as a special celebration.

On the day of Chongyang, people wear twigs from cornel plants. Cornel is a kind of evergreen shrub that blossoms in late spring and early summer and bears fruit in autumn. Its fruit is used in Chinese herbal medicine, its leaves have curative effects against cholera, and its root may serve as an insecticide. From very early on, Chinese people have believed that wearing cornel plants can help them dispel evil and resist the cold weather. The most popular activity during Chongyang is mountain climbing; often entire families go out together to appreciate nature's beauty in this magnificent season and celebrate the family reunion.

The festival of Chongyang is always associated with chrysanthemums. On this day, people drink chrysanthemum wine or chrysanthemum tea and admire the late-year blossoms of chrysanthemums. The chrysanthemum has a very high status in Chinese culture. It is one of the "four gentlemen of plants" (the other three are plum blossoms, orchid, and bamboo). These plants are so called because they are regarded as having certain qualities that a true Chinese gentleman should achieve. In the case of the chrysanthemum, people see integrity, for it blooms at a time when most other flowers have already yielded to the cold, and its stem remains erect even after the flowers have faded. The Chinese have cultivated chrysanthemums for centuries, and today there are numerous varieties, many with unusual colors and shapes. When Chongyang comes, chrysanthemum shows are held in many cities. The beautiful blossoms under the autumn sky attract thousands of admirers. Chrysanthemums are also a symbol of longevity and health.

As *jiu (chiu)*, the Chinese word for "nine," is pronounced the same as the word for "long," Chongyang, a day with double nines, has traditionally been a day for the elderly. Big meals are prepared for them on this day, and all the younger family members come home to wish them happiness and long life.

A Tibetan monk releases a balloon with prayer flags attached at the Jokhang Temple, Tibet's most revered religious structure, at the start of Losar, the Tibetan New Year. Thousands of Tibetans travel to Lhasa, the major city of the region, to celebrate this festival.

7

Four Ethnic Festivals

In addition to the Han, 55 ethnic groups live in China. Each of these minority groups, which together make up less than 10 percent of China's population, has its own distinctive way of life and colorful and unique traditions, including festivals. Given the limited space of this book, it would be impossible to examine the traditional festivals of all 55 minority groups. What follows is but a sampling. Included are four fascinating festivals, each one from a different ethnic group: the Tibetan New Year, the Nadam Fair of the Mongolians, the Torch Festival of the Yi (I), and the Water Splashing Festival of the Dai (Tai).

Tibetan New Year

Some 4.6 million Tibetans inhabit the rugged, snow-clad mountains and high grasslands of western China. This vast, unforgiving area extends across Tibet and into the neighboring provinces of Gansu, Sichuan, Qinghai, and Yunnan. For hundreds of years, Tibetans have sustained themselves in their rigorous environment by hunting, farming, and raising cattle. They live on yak meat, yak butter, and *qingke (ch'ing ko)*, high barley. They drink large quantities of tea to provide their bodies with necessary vitamins and minerals, as vegetables are hard to come by in their land.

The Tibetans are one of the most religious of China's ethnic groups. Their religion, called Lamaism, is a special form of Buddhism that developed from an intermingling of Buddhist teachings and native Tibetan beliefs. In the Tibetan culture, monks known as lamas (Tibetan for "spiritual teachers") are the most respected people. At the top of the religious hierarchy is the Dalai Lama, Tibet's spiritual leader, who is believed to be the reincarnation of the Bodhisattva of Compassion. (The 14th Dalai Lama, born Tenzin Gyatso, has lived in exile in India since 1959, when he fled Tibet in the midst of an uprising against Chinese occupation.)

The most important of the Tibetan festivals is *Losar*, the Tibetan New Year. The Tibetan calendar, a combination of the solar and lunar calendars, is similar to the Chinese lunar calendar in that it is based on 60-year cycles. But the time of Tibetan New Year celebrations varies from area to area. In Lhasa, Tibet's capital, the New Year comes on the first day of the first month on the Tibetan calendar. In some other areas, it falls on the first of the 12th month or the first of the 11th month.

Tibetans have a saying, "New Year is new work," which reflects their recognition that the preparations for Losar require much busy activity. Typically, the food made for Losar includes fresh roasted barley flour, barley wine, tea, butter, mutton, dried yak meat, fried biscuits, fruits, and sweets. Sprouts of wheat or barley are cultivated in buckets of water before the holiday. On the eve of Losar, the young sprouts are placed on the family altar as a symbol of the

A man carries firecrackers through the streets of Lhasa in preparation for the Tibetan New Year.

birth of the New Year. The sprouts also signify a bumper harvest in the New Year. On the last day of the year, after a thorough house-cleaning, people paint auspicious signs on the inner walls of their home with barley flour. Swastikas, which represent indestructible good fortune, are drawn on the outer walls of the house and on the path to the front door. Colorful lamps made from yak butter are a beautiful decoration on the family altar and in the monasteries. People offer various foods to Buddha. They often present a sheep head for good luck.

Like the Han people, Tibetans get together on their New Year's Eve for a family reunion dinner. At this dinner, barley wine, mutton stew, tea, and a special congee (a gruel-like dish) with chunks of barley dough in it are served. Wrapped in the barley dough are little stones, chili peppers, charcoal, or sheep hair, each serving as a prediction of what the coming new year has in store for the person who comes across it during the meal. Stones indicate that the person will be stone-hearted, charcoal signifies that the person will be mean, sheep hair represents kindness, and chili peppers signify a sharp tongue. This is a lighthearted custom—intended more as a joke than a revelation of actual things to come—and people who chew on these objects spit them out right away, to the merriment of all. It is traditional for everybody to have nine servings of the congee, but not to finish any of them. Tibetans believe that doing this will invite good luck and good health for the New Year.

As dawn breaks on New Year's Day, Tibetan housewives rush to fetch the year's first bucket of water, which is called "water of good luck." They burn incense at the water source, tie a scarf around the tap, and set out an offering of sweet barley bread to appease the serpent-beings in the water. The first to return with the water of good luck is considered to have brought the family the most fortune. After drinking and washing in the water of good luck, people light butter lamps in the house and place colored barley plants on pastries to express their hope for a good harvest in the coming year. Family members greet each other with *"Tashi Delek,"* meaning *"good luck to you."* When they visit friends and relatives, they also exchange such greetings. Sometimes they present each other with a white silk scarf called a *hata*, which symbolizes a pure, friendly heart in Tibetan culture.

During the Losar celebrations, everybody dresses in his or her best. Men appear in a loose woolen garment, with the right arm slipped out of the sleeve to show a white undergarment or a woolen sweater inside. They also wear a broad silk sash around the waist, a four-flap hat with golden and silvery threads, and long boots. Women's dresses are even more colorful, accompanied by fancy headgear, leather boots, and beautiful jewelry. A festive atmosphere fills the air during Losar, and everybody seems happy eating, drinking, singing, and dancing.

Mongolian Nadam Fair

The Mongolians are a nomadic people who roam the vast open grasslands of northern China, herding camels, cattle, sheep, and yaks. For hundreds of years, the Mongolians were famous for their military conquests. The powerful armies of Genghis Khan once swept as far west as today's Hungary, and in the 13th century his grandson, Kublai Khan, founded the first non-Han empire to rule the whole of China. Today the Chinese Mongolians number more than 4.8 million; most live in the autonomous region of Inner Mongolia. Their religion, like that of the Tibetans, is Lamaism, whose influence spread as far as Beijing during the Yuan (Yüan) and Qing (Ch'ing) dynasties.

Nadam is the Mongolian word for "recreation." Nadam Fair takes place every year in the seventh or eighth lunar month. This is the most beautiful season on the grassland. The weather is glorious: the sky looks high and the air is crisp. Forage grass grows in profusion, and cattle and sheep are fat and in good form. People put aside their daily affairs and come together on the grassland for a few days of fun and relaxation.

Nadam Fair grew out of celebrations of conquest; in the past, it was often held after victories in war or during political gatherings. Today, it is mostly a sporting festival celebrated with three major activities: wrestling, horse racing, and archery, which the Mongolians call the "men's three events." Nadam Fair lasts from three to seven days, and people come from hundreds of miles around and set up tents at the fair. During the fair, lamas perform rites of sacrifice, lighting incense and lamps and chanting scriptures for Buddha's blessings. Every event at Nadam Fair begins with an elderly man who chants to give the contestants his blessings while holding high a silver bowl filled with fresh milk and a white *hata*.

Wrestling is the favorite sport of the Mongolians, and the wrestling

Mongolian wrestlers compete during the annual Nadam Fair. The main attractions at this event are sporting contests: wrestling, archery, and horse racing.

contest at Nadam Fair is filled with ceremony. Participants wear traditional costumes, including high boots. At the beginning of each match, the contestants perform a wrestler's dance and sing a wrestler's song. According to Mongolian wrestling rules, the contestant loses when any part of his body above the knee touches the ground. The champion of the wrestling contest earns the title "the powerful eagle" and is regarded as the hero of the area.

Mongolians depend heavily on horses in their nomadic way of life on the vast grasslands, and they have a long tradition of horse racing. The Venetian traveler Marco Polo chronicled such events in the 13th century. Today the horse races at Nadam Fair cover scores of miles and attract hundreds of riders. There are two types of horse racing at the Nadam Fair: speed racing and skill racing. The participants in speed racing are usually teenagers, whereas skill racing—in which the horse is not allowed to gallop—is generally reserved for adults.

Today Nadam is not only a sporting festival but also a fair where people exchange merchandise. Makeshift stores and restaurants are set up, and people enjoy great varieties of goods after watching the exciting wrestling, horse racing, and archery contests. In the evening people build bonfires on the grassland, and singing and dancing go on late into the night, with musical accompaniment provided by the *matou qin (ma t'ou ch'in)*, a stringed instrument with a scroll carved like a horse's head.

The Torch Festival

The Yi minority group lives in four provinces in southwestern China: Sichuan, Yunnan, Guizhou, and Guangxi. The group's history dates back as far as the second century B.C. Today the Yi people number more than 6 million.

Each year, on the 24th day of the sixth lunar month (the month of the tiger on the Yi calendar), Yi people everywhere begin to celebrate their Torch Festival. This festival, during which people express their feelings and emotions through fire, usually lasts three days. On the first day, people slaughter oxen and cows for the festival feast. They chop the meat into big chunks and make *tuotuo rou (t'o t'o jou)*, a dish similar to barbecued steak in Western cuisine. On the second day, people dress up in their holiday best. Men wear an embroidered short jacket; a pair of loose, baggy pants; a red or yellow pearl in the right ear; and a blue or black turban with a long "hero's knot" tied near the forehead. Women wear an upper garment embroidered and trimmed with lace, a multifold skirt in variegated colors, and a cloth or a scarf on the head. The main activities during the day are bullfighting, goat fighting, horse racing, and wrestling. People eat *tuotuo rou* and drink corn wine all day long, and they also play music, sing, and dance.

The night of the Torch Festival is enchanting. On the public square of every village, a gigantic torch is erected and lit; smaller torches also burn in front of every house. People gather in open fields on the village outskirts, each holding a burning torch. As hundreds of people with torches move along paths in the fields, the spectacle calls to mind a dancing fire dragon. The most exciting scene on the Torch Festival night is "splashing fire." The celebrants sprinkle an inflammable resin mix over their torches as someone approaches, which causes dazzling flames to shower down on the passerby. The one being "splashed" then chases after them and

Festival-goers watch a horse race during the second day of a Yi Torch Festival in Sichuan Province.

pays them back in the same way. The Yi people believe that these splashing fires can drive away pests and demons.

The legend of the Torch Festival concerns a Yi hero named Eqilaba, who once killed an evil god that had inflicted great pain and disaster on his people. The Heavenly King was not happy about this, and as a punishment he sent swarms of "heavenly insects" to earth to destroy the Yi crops. Eqilaba led people into the mountains, where they cut bamboo for torches, which they used to burn all the insects. The crops were thus saved and the Yi people survived. To commemorate Eqilaba's heroic deeds, and to celebrate man's victory over the insects, people made the burning of torches a ritual. Over time, according to legend, it became the Torch Festival.

The Water Splashing Festival

In southern Yunnan, a province that borders Laos and Cambodia, there is a beautiful tropical rain forest called Sipsongpanna (the "happy land of hope and magic"). A minority group called the Dai (Tai) has inhabited this land for thousands of years. A branch of the Thai people of Thailand, the Dai today number about 1 million. Like their cousins in Thailand, the Dai are Buddhists.

Every year, between the 24th and 26th of the sixth month on the Dai calendar, people celebrate the Water Splashing Festival, the Dai New Year. Long ago, according to legend, there lived a fierce, brutal Demon King in Sipsongpanna. The Demon King had tremendous magic power and brought people great pain. He had seven wives, and they all hated him. One night when the Demon King was drunk, the seven wives managed to find out how he could be killed. When the Demon King fell asleep that night, the seven wives plucked a hair from his head and cut his head off with it. Unfortunately, wherever the head rolled, it started a big fire. People

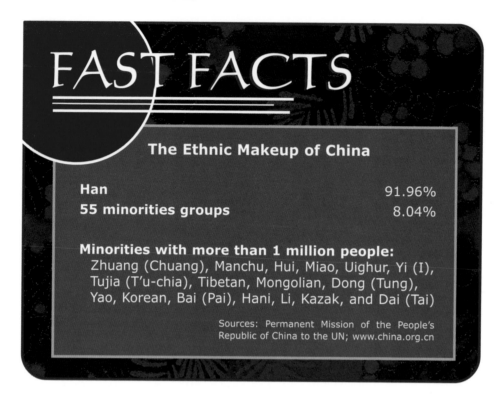

FAST FACTS

The Ethnic Makeup of China

Han	91.96%
55 minorities groups	8.04%

Minorities with more than 1 million people:
Zhuang (Chuang), Manchu, Hui, Miao, Uighur, Yi (I),
Tujia (T'u-chia), Tibetan, Mongolian, Dong (Tung),
Yao, Korean, Bai (Pai), Hani, Li, Kazak, and Dai (Tai)

Sources: Permanent Mission of the People's
Republic of China to the UN; www.china.org.cn

had to splash water on the head for days before they finally ended the disaster. The Water Splashing Festival commemorates the seven brave wives who saved the Dai people from suffering.

The celebrations of the Water Splashing Festival last three to five days. The main activity of the first day is a religious ritual called "bathing the Buddha," which is a ceremonial cleaning of Buddha sculptures. Dragon boat regattas are held on the Lancang (Lants'ang) River, which runs through Sipsongpanna.

The activity of water splashing takes place on the second day. People gather with basins and buckets filled with clean water and splash the water on one another as a way of giving blessings. With the elderly, the custom takes a rather reserved form. The person doing the splashing utters words of good wishes, dips an olive branch into the water, and lets a few drops fall on the elderly person's head; alternatively, the elderly person's collar might be pulled open and a spoonful of water ladled down the spine. With young people, water splashing is much more exciting. They simply throw a basinful or bucketful of water onto each other, and everybody gets wet through and through. It is believed that the more water a person gets splashed with, the more happiness there is for him or her.

During the festival, people also celebrate by dancing peacock dances, setting off firecrackers called *gaosheng (kao sheng)*, and playing *diubao (tiu pao)*, or "throwing pouches." Peacocks thrive in Sipsongpanna, and the Dai people have long developed various art forms to capture the images of these beautiful birds. At a peacock dance, girls dress up in peacock-like costumes and imitate the birds' elegant movements. *Gaosheng* are bamboo tubes stuffed with gunpowder and set on very tall bamboo platforms. When lit, they zoom skyward and produce a whistling sound, symbolizing Dai people's wish for a soaring new year. *Diubao* is an activity for girls and boys. They line up and toss colorful cloth sacks to one another as a throw and catch game. The person who misses a catch gives flowers to the tosser. This is an opportunity for boys and girls to get to know each other, and it adds a romantic atmosphere to the festive celebrations.

Glossary

charm—an item that people wear or use for its supposed magical power.

clan—a large group of people who are descended from a common ancestor.

cosmology—a branch of philosophy dealing with the origin, processes, and structure of the universe.

dualism—the view that the world consists of two fundamental principles.

elixir—a magic potion that can prolong life.

entourage—a group of servants or assistants.

envoy—a representative or a minister with special missions.

exile—the state of being forced to leave one's native country.

kowtow—to kneel down and touch one's forehead to the ground as a salutation.

nostalgia—homesickness; wistful yearning to return to a place or recover a lost way of life.

purgatory—a place of suffering for the dead in the underworld.

regatta—a boat race.

repertoire—the full number of sounds in a language.

taboo—a ban on certain things or activities according to social customs.

Taoism—a major philosophy and religious system of China that promotes non-interference as a way of life. Taoists believe that by studying the Dao (Tao), which literally means "the way," they can attain immortality.

Major Chinese Festivals, Holidays, and Observances

On the Lunar Calendar

First Month

Day 1	Chinese New Year.
Day 9	Birthday of the Jade Emperor, supreme ruler of the Chinese gods.
Day 15	The Lantern Festival.

Second Month

Day 2	Day of the Dragons.
Day 15	Birthday of Laozi (Lao-tzu), founder of Taoism.
Day 19	Birthday of Guanyin (Kuan-yin), the Buddhist Goddess of Mercy.

Third Month

Day 23	Birthday of Tian Hou (T'ien Hou), the Queen of Heaven, who is more commonly known as Mazu (Ma-tsu), Goddess of the Sea, in southeastern China.

Fourth Month

Day 8	Birthday of Sakyamuni, or Gautama Buddha, the founder of Buddhism.

Fifth Month

Day 5	Dragon Boat Festival.

Sixth Month

Day 24   Birthday of Guan Gong (Kuan Kung),
            God of Warriors.

Seventh Month

Day 7   Qiqiao (Ch'i Ch'iao), the Double Seventh;
            annual meeting day of the Weaving Maid
            and the Cowherd.
Day 15   Ghost Festival.
Day 30   Birthday of Dizang Wang (Ti-tsang Wang),
            King of the Underworld, who opens the gates
            of hell and rescues suffering souls.

Eighth Month

Day 15   Mid-Autumn Festival.
Day 27   Birthday of Confucius (551–479 B.C.), China's
            greatest philosopher.

Ninth Month

Day 9   Chongyang (Ch'ung Yang), the Double Ninth.

Tenth Month

Day 1   Sending the Winter Clothes.
Day 5   Birthday of Damo (Ta-mo), or Bodhidharma,
            founder of Chan Buddhism (Zen in Japan).

Twelfth Month

Day 8   Celebration of Sakyamuni achieving enlighten-
            ment. Also known as the day of *laba zhou (la
            pa chou)*, "Gruel of the Eighth Day."

Day 23   Sending off the Kitchen God.

Day 30   Chuxi (Ch'u Hsi), Chinese New Year's Eve.

On the Solar Calendar

January 1   New Year's Day (official holiday in the People's
              Republic of China)

March 8   International Working Women's Day (official
              holiday)

April 4 or 5 Clear Brightness

May 1   International Labor Day (official holiday)

May 4   China Youth Day (official holiday)

June 1   International Children's Day (official holiday)

August 1   Army Day, a celebration of the founding, in
              1927, of the People's Liberation Army (official
              holiday)

October 1   National Day, a celebration of the founding of
              the People's Republic of China in 1949 (official
              holiday)

Dec. 21   Winter solstice

Further Reading

Bredon, Juliet, and Igor Mitrophanow. *The Moon Year: A Record of Chinese Customs and Festivals*. Algonquin, Ill.: Soul Care Publishing, 2009.

Chan, Arlene. *Awakening the Dragon*. Toronto: Tundra Books, 2004.

Han, Carolyn. *The Demon King and Other Festival Folktales of China*. Honolulu: University of Hawaii Press, 1995.

Lai, Kuan Fook. *The Hennessy Book of Chinese Festivals*. Kuala Lumpur: Heineman Asia, 1984.

Latsch, Marie-Luise. *Chinese Traditional Festivals*. Beijing: New World Press, 1984.

Li, Xing. *Festivals of China's Ethnic Minorities*. Beijing: China Intercontinental Press, 2006.

Qi, Xing. *Folk Customs at Traditional Chinese Festivals*. Beijing: Foreign Languages Press, 1988.

Simonds, Nina. *Chinese Seasons*. Boston: Houghton Mifflin, 1986.

Simonds, Nina, and Leslie Swartz. *Moonbeams, Dumplings & Dragon Boats: A Treasury of Chinese Holiday Tales, Activities and Recipes*. San Diego: Harcourt, 2002.

Stepanchuk, Carol. *Red Eggs and Dragon Boats: Celebrating Chinese Festivals*. Berkeley, Calif.: Pacific View Press, 1994.

Stepanchuk, Carol, and Charles Wong. *Mooncakes and Hungry Ghosts: Festivals of China*. San Francisco: China Books & Periodicals, 1991.

Thompson, Stuart, and Angela Dennington. *Chinese Festivals Cookbook*. Austin, Tex.: Raintree Steck-Vaughn Publishers, 2001.

Ward, Barbara E., and Joan Law. *Chinese Festivals in Hong Kong*. San Francisco: China Books and Periodicals, 1993.

Wright, Jeni. *Chinese Food & Folklore*. San Diego: Laurel Glen Publishing, 1999.

Internet Resources

http://chineseculture.about.com/

An online community about China, including articles and links on Chinese history, arts, traditions, music, books, language, literature, and more.

http://www.chinatour.com/countryinfo/festival.htm

Introductions to major festivals celebrated by Chinese all over the world, as well as to festivals celebrated regionally or locally in China.

http://www.paulnoll.com/China/Minorities/index.html

A website devoted to the Chinese national minorities, including descriptions and population as well as beautiful photographs.

http://www.china.org.cn/e-groups/shaoshu/

Basic facts about each of the 56 ethnic groups in China, with pictures and articles about their culture, languages, and history.

Index

Numbers in **bold italics** refer to captions.

Picture Credits

Contributors

YAN LIAO is a native of China. She earned her M.A. in American Studies from Sichuan University, China. Later she studied at the University of Hawai'i and earned an M.A. in English as a Second Language and a Master of Library and Information Science. Currently Yan Liao is an assistant professor at the University of Wisconsin–Stevens Point.

JIANWEI WANG, a native of Shanghai, received his B.A. and M.A. in international politics from Fudan University in Shanghai and his Ph.D. in political science from the University of Michigan. He is now the Eugene Katz Letter and Science Distinguished Professor and chair of the Department of Political Science at the University of Wisconsin–Stevens Point. He is also a guest professor at Fudan University in Shanghai and Zhongshan University in Guangzhou.

Professor Wang's teaching and research interests focus on Chinese foreign policy, Sino-American relations, Sino-Japanese relations, East Asia security affairs, UN peacekeeping operations, and American foreign policy. He has published extensively in these areas. His most recent publications include *Power of the Moment: America and the World After 9/11* (Xinhua Press, 2002), which he coauthored, and *Limited Adversaries: Post-Cold War Sino-American Mutual Images* (Oxford University Press, 2000).

Wang is the recipient of numerous awards and fellowships, including grants from the MacArthur Foundation, Social Science Research Council, and Ford Foundation. He has also been a frequent commentator on U.S.-China relations, the Taiwan issue, and Chinese politics for major news outlets.